52 PROGRAMS FOR PRESCHOOLERS

The Librarian's Year-Round Planner

DIANE BRIGGS

American Library Association
Chicago and London
1997

While extensive effort has gone into ensuring the reliability of information appearing in this book, the publisher makes no warranty, express or implied, on the accuracy or reliability of the information, and does not assume and hereby disclaims any liability to any person for any loss or damage caused by errors or omissions in this publication.

The paper used in this publication meets the minimum requirements of American National Standard for Information Sciences—Permanence of Paper for Printed Library Materials, ANSI Z39.48-1992. ∞

Cover design by Baugher Design

Text design by Dianne Rooney and Connie Richardson

Composition in Tekton and ITC Garamond
using QuarkXPress 3.3 by the dotted i

Printed on 60-pound Victor Offset, a pH-neutral stock, and
bound in 10-point coated cover stock by Victor Graphics

Library of Congress Cataloging-in-Publication Data

Briggs, Diane.
    52 programs for preschoolers : the librarian's year-round planner /
Diane Briggs.
        p.   cm.
    Includes bibliographical references.
    ISBN 0-8389-0705-9 (alk. paper)
    1. Storytelling—United States.   2. Children's libraries—Activity
programs—United States.   3. Libraries—Services to preschool
children—United States.   I. Title.
Z718.3.B75   1997
027.62′51—dc21   96-52415

Printed in the United States of America.

01   5   4

To my son, Thomas,
and to
Brian, Jessica, and Sarah

CONTENTS

ACKNOWLEDGMENTS

I would like to thank the youth services staff of the Bethlehem Public Library. While working with this remarkably creative group of people over the years, I acquired much of the knowledge needed to produce this book. Particularly, I'd like to thank them for the ideas that I have used, either in whole or in part, to design the following programs: "Happy New Year," "Reach for Peace" (Martin Luther King Day), "Stuffed-Animal Pet Show," and "The Mad Hatter's Tea Party." Kind thanks go to Lisa Bouchard for permission to use "Five Clever Leprechauns" flannel board poem and "Mad Tea Party" skit. I'd also like to thank Lisa Renz of the Troy Public Library for permission to use the "Monkey See, Monkey Do" action rhyme and for showing me her wonderful collection of finger puppets that helped me to form ideas for this book. The rest of the finger plays, action rhymes, and songs contained in this book were either collected from traditional folklore by unknown authors or written by myself unless otherwise indicated. Every effort has been made to find unknown authors, and any copyright omission or credit not given is unintentional. Much thanks to my editor Patrick Hogan for his help and guidance. Finally, I would like to thank my husband, Scott, for the tremendous help and support he gave me while I worked on this project.

INTRODUCTION

Children's librarians know the magic of a successful storytime. The joy in the eyes of the children is reward enough. For those who don't get to see that glow, point to rising circulation rates as an added benefit. Maybe the proud parents are Friends in the making. Few question the long-range benefits. Good times develop good feelings for reading and for libraries, and children will grow up to be taxpayers.

The problem in children's programming is time. I know the crunch. In more than ten years as a children's librarian, I have put together countless programs. This book will help you save time by doing the planning for you, year-round. I have assembled the building blocks for 52 programs organized by theme. To bring in the audience, each program includes a ready-to-use publicity blurb appropriate for public service announcements on radio or television or in newspapers, fliers, or your library Web site. The programs feature recommended books, finger plays, music, flannel board patterns, finger puppets, video recommendations, and craft activities. All in all, there is more than you can use in one storytime session. You will choose what you love best, and that's the way to make the magic happen at your library.

PUBLICITY

Brief publicity notices for fliers, newspapers, radio, public-access television, or a library Internet home page are included with each program. Use them as they are or change them to suit your needs.

CHOOSING BOOKS

The primary goal or aim of a storytime program is to share wonderful high-quality books with children. To that end, I have selected from the best of children's literature when compiling the book lists for each theme. Complete information for these titles appears in the bibliography at the back of the book. I have deliberately listed more books than you can read during one storytime session so you will have a selection to choose from. In my storytimes I usually share approximately three to four books, depending on the length of each. The rest of the time I easily fill with related activities such as finger plays, songs, or a craft. Read only the books that you enjoy and your enthusiasm will come across to the children.

FINGER PLAYS AND ACTION RHYMES

Mothers have been doing finger plays with their children for centuries. Friedrich Froebel, the "father of the kindergarten," recognized the value of this tradition and incorporated finger plays into his kindergarten curriculum. He once said,

> What the child imitates, he begins to understand. Let him represent the flying of birds, and he enters partially into the life of birds. Let him imitate the rapid motion of fishes in the water, and his sympathy with fishes is quickened. . . . In one word let him reflect in his play the varied aspects of life and his thought will begin to grapple with their significance.[1]

Beyond that, children love finger plays and have a delightful time doing them over and over again. When doing a finger play with children, you may want to repeat it three or four times. The first time is like a demonstration; the second time, encourage them to join in. Once they have learned it,

they usually will want to do it at least one more time. Finger plays and action rhymes work as transitions between stories, like a glue that holds a storytime program together. When you do finger plays with children you are perpetuating a wonderful folk tradition.

MUSIC

Always try to include music in your storytimes whether you choose to sing, play a musical instrument, or play recorded music. Songs invigorate a program. Children may join in if they know the song, or you can repeat a song to help them learn it.

Many of the songs in this book have basic chords for guitar or autoharp. It might be worthwhile to dust off that old guitar or tune up the autoharp and add a musical element to your storytime. The autoharp is easy for anyone to play. Just push the button for a designated chord and strum. Lullabies sound wonderful on the autoharp. For your convenience, all song tunes are listed in the discography at the end of the book.

Another great way to bring music into your program is to play recorded background music while you read a story. In his book *Musical Story Hours,* William Painter gives numerous suggestions for combining classical music with picture books and puppetry.[2] Begin and end your storytimes with familiar "hello" and "goodbye" songs and try to include the children's names if possible. Sing lullabies or quiet songs to calm or relax a group. Use songs that require action or movement during the middle part of the program to help release pent-up energy.

FLANNEL BOARD STORYTELLING

You can easily make flannel boards, sometimes also referred to as "felt boards," out of a rectangle of plywood, foamboard, or heavy cardboard. The size should be 34 inches wide by 24 inches high or dimensions close to that. Cover the board with flannel or felt, and you're ready to tell stories.

How to Make Story Figures

Felt is the most attractive medium to use when making story figures. You can also use Pellon and nonfusable interfacing, which are easy to color or paint. These fabrics can be found in craft or fabric stores. Following are some tips for making story figures with felt.

1. Photocopy the story figures and enlarge them to fit your flannel board. Then trace around the patterns on felt.
2. Use different colors for each piece of clothing or detail (face, hair, etc.)
3. Use a flexible fabric glue. If you use other types of glue, your figures may fall apart.
4. For eyes, glue on beads, googly eyes, or paper eyes.
5. Use a permanent black felt-tip pen to help indicate details. Test your pen on a scrap of felt first to get the desired effect and to make sure it doesn't bleed.
6. Use craft hair, sequins, beads, craft feathers, and other interesting materials to decorate your story figures.

FINGER PUPPETS

An easy way to include puppetry in your storytimes is by using finger puppets. They dramatize and enliven simple poems, and you can make them enter or exit by folding down your fingers or by hiding your hand behind your back. Use Velcro pieces to attach felt or posterboard puppets to a glove. Any solid color glove will do. Inexpensive brown cotton work gloves will work well. Patterns are provided with the finger-puppet poems in this book.

VIDEOS

Videos have become a part of most public library collections. The best of this genre should be occasionally featured during storytime programs. Short videos fit nicely into a half hour or forty-five minute storytime program. The titles cited in this book range from about five to fifteen minutes in length.

CRAFTS

The craft projects suggested use easily obtainable materials. Some preparation may be required for a project. Use washable markers unless permanent markers are specified.

Notes

1. Friedrich Froebel, *Mother-Play and Nursery Songs,* Boston: Lothrup, 1873, 1906.
2. William Painter, *Musical Story Hours: Using Music with Storytelling and Puppetry,* Hamden, Conn.: Library Professional Publ., 1989.

PART ONE

CELEBRATIONS

Happy New Year!

PUBLICITY

Preschoolers and parents or caregivers, come join us on _____ at
the_____ Library for a glittering New Year's Eve celebration.
Wear your fancy party clothes and bring a favorite snack to share. We will
have stories, songs, a New Year's Eve countdown (just before noon), and
more. Call _____ to register.

BOOK SUGGESTIONS

Baker, Alan. *Benjamin's Balloon*.
Clifton, Lucille. *Three Wishes*.
Lewis, Paul Owen. *P. Bear's New
    Years Party!*

Modell, Frank. *Goodbye Old Year,
    Hello New Year*.

SONG/DANCE

The Hokey Pokey

Play a recording of the song and have children sing along while doing the dance actions. The song can be found on the *Dancin' Magic* album by Discovery Music (1991).

GAME

Musical Carpet Squares

Musical Carpet Squares is the same as musical chairs except that carpet squares are used instead of chairs. Arrange the carpet squares in a circle or an oblong, start the music, and you're ready to play.

SONG

Auld Lang Syne

Should auld acquaintance be forgot,
And never brought to mind?
Should auld acquaintance be forgot,
And days of Auld Lang Syne?

Chorus

> For Auld Lang Syne, my dear,
> For Auld Lang Syne,
> We'll take a cup of kindness yet
> For Auld Lang Syne!
> —Robert Burns

ACTIVITY

Countdown

Do a countdown just before noon. At noon throw confetti, release balloons, and sing "Auld Lang Syne."

CRAFT

Noisemakers

Let the children create noisemakers using paper towel tubes. To prepare the craft, punch a few holes in the tubes. This will produce somewhat different notes when children hold their fingers over the holes while blowing. Next, let the children decorate the tubes by gluing on confetti and sequins. They can glue crepe paper streamers to the end of the tube. Now, encourage them to hum, toot, or sing through the tube!

Supplies

sequins or confetti
paper towel tubes
glue sticks
crepe paper

Hearts
and
Flowers

PUBLICITY

Preschoolers and parents or caregivers, come to the _____
Library on _____ and enjoy the warmth of Valentine's Day. We will
have stories, songs, a short video, and a craft activity. Call _____
to register.

BOOK SUGGESTIONS

Brett, Jan. *The Owl and the Pussycat*.

Brown, Marc. *Arthur's Valentine*.

Bunting, Eve. *The Valentine Bears*.

Carrick, Carol. *Valentine*.

Cohen, Miriam. *Bee My Valentine!*

Hurd, Thacher. *Little Mouse's Big Valentine*.

Modell, Frank. *One Zillion Valentines*.

FINGER PLAYS

Lots of Valentines

I've made a lot of valentines,
*(trace the shape of a heart in the
air)*
On this February day.
Red ones, pink ones, blue ones,
All to give away.
(pretend to give away valentines)
Some of them have cupids,
(pretend to use bow and arrow)
Some of them have bows,
(pretend to tie a bow)
Some of them have tiny hearts
(trace heart in air)
And this one has a rose.
(cup hands like a flower)

Chocolates

Chocolates in a box all shut up
tight.
(cover one hand with the other)
Down in the dark without any light.
Open the box and what a delight!
(lift hand)
Caramels, creams, nuts, and jellies.
All right!
Mmmm. Good!
(pretend to eat chocolates)

SONG

Lavender's Blue

   D   G
Lavender's blue, dilly, dilly, lavender's green;
   D   A7   D
When I am King, dilly, dilly, you shall be queen.
   D   G
Who told you so, dilly, dilly, who told you so?
   D   A7   D
'Twas my own heart, dilly, dilly, that told me so.

—English Traditional Song

FLANNEL BOARD POEM

Five Gay Valentines

Five gay valentines from the ten cent store.
I sent one to mother, now there are four.
Four gay valentines, pretty ones to see.
I gave one to brother, now there are three.
Three gay valentines, the yellow, red, and blue.
I gave one to sister, now there are two.
Two gay valentines, my we have fun.
I gave one to daddy, now there is one.
One gay valentine, the story is almost done,
I gave it to baby, and now there is none.

Directions

Enlarge the patterns on a photo-copier and make the figures out of felt. Place all the valentines on the flannel board. Remove them one by one as you say the poem. For tips on making flannel board figures, see the section on flannel board story-telling in the introduction.

VIDEO

Show "The Owl and the Pussycat" on the video *Happy Birthday Moon and Other Stories* from Children's Circle (12 minutes).

CRAFT

Valentine Cards

Provide the children with construction paper, paper doilies, stickers, glitter, shiny paper, washable markers, and glue and let them create.

Reach for Peace
(Martin Luther King Day)

PUBLICITY

In honor of Martin Luther King Day, preschoolers and their parents or caregivers are invited to join us in a celebration of brotherhood and goodwill at the _____ Library on _____.
Featured will be stories about friendship, fellowship, and working together. Leave a message of goodwill in our "Goodwill Soup" pot and have fun helping to make a special "Reach for Peace" banner that will be displayed in the library. Call _____ to register.

BOOK SUGGESTIONS

Carle, Eric. *Do You Want to Be My Friend?*

Delton, Judy. *Two Good Friends*.

Hutchins, Pat. *My Best Friend*.

Kellogg, Steven. *The Island of the Skog*.

Lionni, Leo. *Little Blue and Little Yellow*.

Raschka, Chris. *Yo! Yes?*

Seuss, Dr. *The Sneeches and Other Stories*.

13

ACTION RHYME

Friends Come Play with Me

Come play with me at my house,
(beckon with hand)
It's raining out today.
(flutter fingers down)
I'll show you my pet mouse,
(cup hands as if holding mouse)
But don't let him get away.
(shake head)

We'll make some paper airplanes,
(pretend to fold)
And fly them in the house.
(pretend to throw an airplane)
And maybe for a pilot,
We can use my little mouse.

FINGER PUPPETS

Come on, Friends

Come on, little friends, and take a
walk with me.
Come on, frog, jump off your log.
Come on, kitten, put on your
mittens.
Come on, bear, come out of your
lair.
Come on, bunny, you're such
a honey.
Come on, bee, come with
me.
I like my friends, each and
every one.
Because every day we have so
much fun.

Directions

Use the patterns provided here to make five puppets out of felt. Attach Velcro to the back of the puppets and to the fingers of a glove. Start the rhyme with your fingers folded down and raise them one at a time as you say the rhyme.

SONGS

The More We Get Together

```
        D                    A7       D
The more we get together, together, together,
                           A7          D
The more we get together, the happier we'll be,
      A7            D
Cause your friends are my friends,
      A7           D
And my friends are your friends,
                         A7          D
The more we get together, the happier we'll be.
```

—Traditional

Buddies and Pals

The song "Buddies and Pals" can be found in *Do Your Ears Hang Low?* by Tom Glazer. The musical arrangement and guitar chords are included.

16

 CELEBRATIONS

ACTIVITY

Goodwill Soup

As they enter the program area, ask each family to write a brief message of goodwill on a slip of paper and place it in a "Goodwill Soup" pot. Upon leaving the program area, each family will be asked to take a message of goodwill out of the pot.

VIDEO

Show *The Island of the Skog* from Children's Circle (12 minutes).

CRAFT

Reach for Peace Banner

Help each child place the palm of one hand in tempera paint and then make a handprint on a cloth banner made from a white sheet. Write the name of each child in permanent marker under each hand print. This is best done near an area with a sink so that the children can immediately wash their hands. Display the banner in the library under the heading "Reach for Peace."

Supplies

tempera paint (several colors)
paper towels (to wipe hands)
sheet
permanent markers

Groundhog Day!

PUBLICITY

Celebrate Groundhog Day with us at the _____
Library on _____. We'll have great groundhog stories, funny
finger plays, and silly songs. Make a pop-up groundhog puppet to take
home. Call _____ to register. Preschoolers, ages 3–6.

BOOK SUGGESTIONS

Balian, Lorna. *A Garden for a Groundhog.*

Cohen, Carol L. *Wake Up, Groundhog.*

Kroll, Steven. *It's Groundhog Day!*

Tompert, Ann. *Nothing Sticks Like a Shadow.*

Watson, Wendy. *Has Winter Come?*

FINGER PLAYS

Groundhog in His Hole

A groundhog lived in a little hole,
(hold up fist with thumb tucked inside)
Lived quietly in a little hole.
When all was quiet as quiet can be . . .
Out popped he!
(pop up thumb)

The Groundhog

There was a little groundhog,
(hold up thumb)
He lived in a hole.
(tuck thumb in fist)
He lived there all winter long,
With his little friend the mole.
(wiggle pinky)
He stuck his little head up,
(pop up thumb)
To see if it was spring,
And when he didn't see his shadow,
He began to dance and sing.
(wiggle thumb)
For if a groundhog sees his shadow,
It means winter is not done,
(tuck thumb in fist)
But if he doesn't see his shadow
It's time for springtime fun!
(hold up thumb and wiggle it)

FINGER PUPPETS

Five Little Groundhogs

Five little groundhogs on Groundhog Day,
The first one said, "I'll have a peek if I may."
The second one said, "Is it warm or cold?"
The third one said, "Let's get out of this hole."
The fourth one said, "Is that a shadow I see?"
The fifth one said, "No, it's only me."
When the groundhogs popped their heads out,
No shadows did they see.
"Spring is finally here!" they shouted.
"And we're free, free, free!!!"

Directions

Use the pattern to make five ground-hogs out of felt. Attach Velcro to the back of each one and to the fingers of a glove.

SONG

Groundhog Song

(Tune: "My Bonnie Lies Over the Ocean")

The little groundhog saw his shadow.
It was cast on the ground by the sun.
The little groundhog went back under,
Because cold wintertime was not done.

CRAFT

Pop-Up Groundhog Puppet

Prior to the program, poke a hole in the bottom center of a paper cup. Let children glue or tape a ground-hog picture to the end of a drinking straw and slide the other end of the straw through the hole in the cup. This puppet may be used with the groundhog finger plays and song.

Supplies

pictures of groundhogs
paper cups
straws
tape

Leaping Leprechauns!

PUBLICITY

Join us in celebration of St. Patrick's Day at the _____
Library on _____. Come wearin' the green and we'll have
stories, songs, and a leprechaun hunt. Enjoy creating a leprechaun stick
puppet to take home. Call _____ to register. Preschoolers,
ages 3–6.

BOOK SUGGESTIONS

Bunting, Eve. *St. Patrick's Day in the Morning.*

Chute, Linda. *Clever Tom and the Leprechaun.*

De Paola, Tomie. *Fin M'Cool: The Giant of Knockmany Hill.*

———. *Jamie O'Rourke and the Big Potato.*

McDermott, Gerald. *Tim O'Toole and the Wee Folk.*

FLANNEL BOARD POEM

Five Clever Leprechauns

Five clever leprechauns, all dressed in green,
The first one said, "We mustn't be seen!"
The second one said, "Should we hide our pot of
    gold?"
The third one said, "That's what I've been told!"
The fourth one said, "Look! I see a rainbow!"
And the fifth one said, "Well, come on! Let's go!"
Then all of those little people ran away,
Do you know why? It was St. Patrick's Day!

—Lisa Bouchard

Directions

Make five felt leprechauns with the
pattern provided. Add green
sequins to the leprechauns and
gold sequins to the pot of gold.
Place the leprechauns on the flannel board one by one as you say
the poem. Remove them at the end
of the poem.

SONG

Too-ra-loo-ra

Too-ra-loo-ra-loo-ral
Too-ra-loo-ra-li
Too-ra-loo-ra-loo-ral
Hush now, don't you cry.

Too-ra-loo-ra-loo-ral
Too-ra-loo-ra-li
Too-ra-loo-ra-loo-ral
That's an Irish lullaby.

ACTIVITY

Dance a Jig

Play Irish music, form a circle, and dance the jig. Have children place their hands on their hips and hop alternately on each foot.

GAME

Leprechaun Hunt

Before the children arrive, hide cutouts of leprechauns, shamrocks, and pots of gold around the room. Let the children search for them. Count the objects together when they are all found.

CRAFT

Leprechaun Stick Puppet

Let the children glue googly eyes, yarn hair, and precut construction paper clothing to tongue depressors. They can use markers to draw on mouths and noses and glue on green glitter or sequins.

Supplies

green construction paper
tongue depressors or craft sticks
yarn for hair
googly eyes
glitter
sequins
glue

May Day

PUBLICITY

Preschoolers and their parents or caregivers are invited to a May Day celebration at the _____ Library on _____.
We'll have spring stories, do a flower craft, and sing May Day songs while we dance around the Maypole. Call _____ to register.

BOOK SUGGESTIONS

Alexander, Sue. *There's More . . . Much More.*
Bunting, Eve. *Flower Garden.*
Delton, Judy. *Three Friends Find Spring.*

Minarik, Else. *It's Spring!*
Rockwell, Anne. *My Spring Robin.*
Wells, Rosemary. *Forest of Dreams.*

FINGER PLAYS

Flowers Grow

This is the way the flowers sleep,
    (make fists of both hands)
Through the winter long.
This is the way the flowers grow,
    (open hands)
When they hear the robin's song.
    (raise arms)

During Spring

During spring it often showers,
    (flutter fingers down)
Or the sun shines for many hours,
    (form circle in the air with arms)
Both are good for flowers.
    (cup hands and extend arms up)

Houses

Here is a nest for robin,
    (cup hands)
Here is a hive for bee,
    (put fists together)
Here is a hole for bunny,
    (form a circle with hands)
And here is a house for me.
    (form a peak overhead with hands)

ACTION RHYME

Here Is a Bunny

Here is a bunny
    (hold up two fingers)
With ears so funny.
    (wiggle fingers)
Here is his hole in the ground.
    (make a circle with arms to indicate hole)
When a noise he hears,
He pricks up his ears,
    (straighten fingers)
And jumps in his hole in the ground.
    (pretend to jump in hole)

SONGS

Nuts in May

(*Tune:* "Here We Go 'Round the Mulberry Bush")

Here we come gathering nuts in May,
Nuts in May, nuts in May,
Here we come gathering nuts in May,
All on a sunny morning.

Here we come gathering flowers in May . . .

Here we go 'round the Maypole . . .

Around the Maypole

(*Tune:* "London Bridge")

Around the Maypole here we go,
Here we go, here we go,
Around the Maypole here we go,
All on a May Day morning.

ACTIVITY

Dance around Maypole

Attach flowers and streamers to a pole. An indoor free-standing flag-pole will work well, but you may need to anchor its base with weights. Give each child a streamer. Dance around the pole as you sing "Nuts in May," "Around the Maypole," or any other song that you like. Reverse directions when the streamers get short and do it all over again.

VIDEO

Frog and Toad are Friends, distributed by Churchill (30 minutes), contains several short segments. Show "Spring," which is five minutes long.

CRAFT

Tissue Paper Flowers

Prior to the program, fold several layers of 5″ × 8″ tissue paper in an accordion pattern and twist a green pipe cleaner around the middle of the folded paper. Demonstrate how to separate the layers of tissue paper. Give each child a prefolded flower and let him or her separate the layers to create a flower.

Supplies

green pipe cleaners
tissue paper of various colors

I Love You, Mom!

PUBLICITY

Moms and preschoolers are invited to a Mother's Day storytime at the
_____ Library on _____. Join us for
stories, songs, finger plays, and a fun craft. Call _____
to register.

BOOK SUGGESTIONS

Bunting, Eve. *The Mother's Day Mice.*

Butterworth, Nick. *My Mom Is Excellent.*

Joosse, Barbara M. *Mama, Do You Love Me?*

Morris, Ann. *The Mommy Book.*

Munsch, Robert. *Love You Forever.*

Polushkin, Maria. *Mother, Mother, I Want Another.*

Porter-Gaylord, Laurel. *I Love My Mommy Because.*

Smalls, Irene. *Jonathan and His Mommy.*

Waddell, Martin. *The Big, Big Sea.*

ACTION RHYME

My Mom

My mom is very special,
I think that you'll agree,
She picks the greatest stories
(hold palms out, pretend to read)
To read aloud to me.
Sometimes we go fishing,
(pretend to cast out line)
Or play a game of ball.
(pretend to hit a ball, use sound effects)
She always gives me great big hugs,
(hug self)
She's the best mom of them all!

FINGER PLAYS

Here Is the Little Girl

Here is the little girl (or boy) ready
for her nap,
(hold up one finger)
Lay her down in her mommy's lap.
(lay finger in palm)
Cover her up, so she won't peep,
(close hand over finger)
Rock her 'til she's fast asleep.
(rock hands back and forth)

(*Note:* This song may also be used for Father's Day. Change "mommy" to "daddy.")

At Night I See the Twinkling Stars

At night I see the twinkling stars,
(open and shut hands to indicate twinkling stars)
And a great big smiling moon.
(encircle arms overhead)
My mommy tucks me into bed,
(pretend to tuck child in bed)
And sings a good-night tune.
(sing a lullaby)

SONG

Special Mommy

(*Tune:* Oscar Mayer "I Wish I Were an Oscar Mayer Wiener" theme song)

Have you ever seen such a special mommy?
She plays with me and loves me all the time.
Have you ever seen such a special mommy?
I sure am very happy that she's mine.

(*Note:* This song may also be used for Father's Day. Change "mommy" to "daddy.")

VIDEO

"Blueberries for Sal" can be found on the video *The Robert McCloskey Library*, Children's Circle (10 minutes).

CRAFT

Queen-for-a-Day Crown

Provide the moms and preschoolers with poster-board crowns to decorate. Distribute crayons, markers, glue, beads, sequins, and let them create.

Supplies

crayons or washable markers
poster board
sequins
beads
glue

I Love You, Dad!

PUBLICITY

Dads and preschoolers are invited to a Father's Day storytime at the
_____ Library on _____. Listen
to dad stories, sing dad songs, and play a fun ring-toss game. Call
_____ to register.

BOOK SUGGESTIONS

Asch, Frank. *Just Like Daddy*.

Bunting, Eve. *A Perfect Father's Day*.

Carle, Eric. *Papa, Please Get the
Moon for Me*.

McPhail, David. *Emma's Pet*.

Morris, Ann. *The Daddy Book*.

Sharmat, Marjorie. *Hooray for
Father's Day*.

FINGER PLAY

Here's the Boy

Here is the little boy (or girl) ready
for his nap,
(hold up one finger)
Lay him down in his daddy's lap,
(lay fingers in palm)
Cover him up, so he won't peep,
(close hand over finger)
Rock him 'til he's fast asleep.
(rock hands back and forth)

SONG

My Daddy Is Really Quite Special

(*Tune:* "My Bonnie Lies over the
Ocean")

    D   G   D
My daddy is really quite special
             G   A7
My daddy is really quite fine
    D   G
He hugs me, and helps me, and
     D
   loves me,
   G   A7   D
I'm so very glad that he's mine.
    D   G
Oh Daddy, Oh Daddy
 A7   D
You are the greatest to me, to me!
    D   G
Oh Daddy, Oh Daddy
 A7   D
You are the greatest to me!

(*Note:* This song may also be used
for Mother's Day. Change "daddy" to
"mommy.")

ACTION RHYME

My Dad

My dad is very special,
I think that you'll agree,
He picks the greatest stories
    (hold out palms, pretend to read)
To read aloud to me.
Sometimes we go fishing,
    (pretend to cast out line)
Or play a game of ball.
    *(pretend to hit a ball, use sound
     effects)*
He always gives me great big hugs,
    (hug self)
He's the best dad of them all!

CRAFT

Ring Toss

Prior to the program, fasten paper
towel tubes to cardboard rectangles
and make rings with pipe cleaners,
two pipe cleaners for each ring.
Invite children to try to toss the rings
over the paper towel tubes.

Supplies

cardboard
paper towel tubes
pipe cleaners

It's a Birthday Party!

PUBLICITY

Preschoolers, bring your favorite stuffed animal or doll to the _____ Library on _____. We will celebrate their birthdays with stories, songs, cake decorating, and more. Call _____ to register.

BOOK SUGGESTIONS

Argent, Kerry. *Happy Birthday, Wombat!*

Carle, Eric. *The Secret Birthday Message.*

Inkpen, Mick. *Kipper's Birthday.*

Robart, Rose. *The Cake That Mack Ate.*

Spurr, Elizabeth. *The Biggest Birthday Cake in the World.*

Tafuri, Nancy. *The Barn Party.*

Yolen, Jane. *Mouse's Birthday.*

ACTION RHYME

A Birthday Cake

Let's have a birthday party,
Let's make a birthday cake;
 (form a circle with arms)
Mix and stir, stir and mix,
 (stirring motions)
Then into the oven to bake.
 (pretend to put cake in oven)
Here's our cake so nice and round,
 (form a circle with arms)
We'll frost it pink and white;
 (pretend to frost)
We'll put five candles on it,
 (hold up five fingers)
And light the birthday light.
 (pretend to light candles)
And then, blow them out!
 (blow out imaginary candles)

FINGER PLAY

Blow up a Balloon

Here's a balloon without any air,
Flimsy as can be.
 (pretend to shake an empty
  balloon)
What happens when we blow it up?
Let's try it out and see . . .
 (hold hands together in front of
  face)
With a huff and a puff,
And a great big blow,
 (pretend to blow up balloon)
It gets bigger and bigger,
Just watch it grow.
 (slowly move hands wide apart
  while blowing)

SONG

Happy Birthday to You

Play "Happy Birthday to You" from Sharon, Lois, and Bram's *Happy Birthday* album. Other songs on this album are also appropriate.

FINGER PUPPETS

Cupcakes

Five little cupcakes in a bakery shop,
Round and fat with frosting on top.
Along came _____ (child's
 name) with her quarter one day.
And bought a cupcake and ran away.
Four little cupcakes . . .
Three little cupcakes . . .
Two little cupcakes . . .
One little cupcake...

Directions

Use the pattern to make five cupcakes out of felt. You may want to
change the facial expression for each
one. Attach Velcro to the back of
each cupcake and to the fingers of a
glove. Use a hand puppet to remove
the cupcakes, one at a time, as you
say the rhyme.

VIDEO

Show *Happy Birthday Moon,* distributed by Weston Woods (7 minutes).

ACTIVITY

Cake Decorating

Give each child a cupcake to decorate. Distribute several small bowls
of frosting and a variety of cake dec-
orations. Tongue depressors may be
used to spread the frosting.

Boo!

PUBLICITY

Preschoolers, wear your Halloween costumes and come to the
_____ Library on _____ for ghostly tales,
a pumpkin game, Halloween tunes, and a parade through the library. Make
a furry bat to take home. Please call _____ to register.

BOOK SUGGESTIONS

Andrews, Sylvia. *Rattlebone Rock.*

Bender, Robert. *A Little Witch Magic.*

Enderle, Judith Ross. *Six Creepy Sheep.*

Martin, Bill. *Old Devil Wind.*

Roberts, Bethany. *Halloween Mice.*

Silverman, Erica. *Big Pumpkin.*

Ziefert, Harriet. *In a Scary Old House.*

ACTION RHYME

A Little Witch

A little witch in a pointed cap
    (make cap on head with hands)
On my door went rap, rap, rap.
    (do rapping motion)
When I went to open it,
    *(pretend to open door, use
      squeaking sound effects)*
She was not there.
She was riding on a broomstick,
    *(put right fist on left wrist and
      move left arm upward quickly)*
High up in the air.

FINGER PLAY/PUPPET

Mr. Pumpkin

Old Mr. Pumpkin
Hiding in a box,
    *(make a fist with right hand,
      cover fist with left hand)*
Take off the top,
    (remove left hand)
And out he pops.
    (pop up thumb)

(*Alternative:* Make a little pumpkin finger puppet out of felt or poster board to wear on your thumb.)

GAME

Pass the Pumpkin

Form a circle and sit cross legged on the floor. Play Halloween music and pass a small pumpkin around the circle. When the music stops, whoever is holding the pumpkin receives a small prize or treat.

ACTION RHYME/SONG

Orange Pumpkin

(*Tune:* "I'm a Little Teapot")

I'm an orange pumpkin,
Fat and round,
    *(hold arms out to indicate
      roundness)*
Sitting in the cornfield
On the ground.
I'll be a jack-o'-lantern,
With two big eyes.
    (circle eyes with fingers)
Or made into a big fat pie.
    (make pie shape with arms)

OVERHEAD PROJECTOR STORY

Witches' Brew

Put a glass pie plate filled with water on an overhead projector. Add the ingredients while saying the ingenious witches' brew chant found on page 159 in *When the Lights Go Out: Twenty Scary Tales to Tell* by Margaret Read MacDonald.

Supplies

glass pie plate with water
food coloring
salad oil
yarn
thread
sharp pebble
Bromo Seltzer crystals or crushed
    Alka Seltzer tablets

VIDEO

Show "What's under My Bed" on *What's under My Bed and Other Creepy Stories* from Children's Circle (10 minutes).

CRAFT

Furry Bat on a Stick

Supply each child with a bat silhouette made of thin black poster board or heavy stock paper. Let the children glue pieces of craft fur on the bats. Sequins or beads may be glued on for eyes. Staple or tape cut rubber bands to the bats. Tape the other end of the rubber band to a craft stick.

Supplies

black poster board or heavy paper
sequins or beads
rubber bands
craft sticks
craft fur
glue
stapler

Giving
Thanks

PUBLICITY

Thanksgiving is almost here. At the _____
Library on _____ we will tell stories, sing songs, and make
miniature turkeys. Join us for a delightful time! Call _____ to
register. Preschoolers, ages 3–6.

BOOK SUGGESTIONS

Accorsi, William. *Friendship's First
    Thanksgiving.*
Bunting, Eve. *A Turkey for
    Thanksgiving.*
Child, Lydia Maria. *Over the River
    and through the Wood.*
Nicola-Lisa, W. *1, 2, 3, Thanksgiving.*

Stock, Catherine. *Thanksgiving
    Treat.*
Swamp, Chief Jake. *Giving Thanks:
    A Native American Good
    Morning Message.*

FINGER PLAYS

The Turkey Is a Funny Bird

The turkey is a funny bird,
*(make a fist and extend thumb,
place the palm of the other hand
against the side of your fist
opposite the thumb, your
extended fingers represent the
feathers)*
His head goes wobble, wobble.
(wag thumb)
He only knows a single word:
Gobble, gobble, gobble.
(wag thumb again)

Our Turkey

Our turkey is a big fat bird,
(hold hands far apart)
He gobbles when he talks.
*(open and close hand to indicate
gobbling)*
His long red chin is drooping down,
(cup hand under chin)
He waddles when he walks.
*(move hands up and down
alternately)*
His tail is like a spreading fan
(spread fingers of one hand)
On Thanksgiving Day—
He spreads his tail high in the air
And whooooosh—he flies away!
(shoot hand into air)

SONG

Over the River and through the Wood

Over the river and through the
wood
To Grandmother's house we go.
The horse knows the way
To carry the sleigh
Through the white and drifted snow.

Over the river and through the
wood
Oh how the wind does blow.
It stings the toes and bites the nose
As over the fields we go.

Over the river and through the
wood
Trot fast my dapple gray.
Spring over the ground
Like hunting hound
For this is Thanksgiving Day.

Over the river and through the
wood
Now Grandmother's cap I spy.
Hooray for the fun
Is the pudding done?
Hooray for the pumpkin pie!
—Traditional

FLANNEL BOARD POEM

Five Little Pilgrims

Five little pilgrims on Thanksgiving
    Day,
The first one said, "I'll have cake if I
    may."
The second one said, "I'll have a
    turkey roasted."
The third one said, "I'll have chest-
    nuts toasted."

The fourth one said, "I'll have a
    pumpkin pie."
The fifth one said, "Oh, cranberries I
    spy."
But before the pilgrims ate their
    turkey dressing,
They bowed their heads and gave a
    Thanksgiving blessing.

Directions

Enlarge the patterns on a photo-copier and make five pilgrims. Place the pilgrims on the flannel board before you say the poem. Add the cake, turkey, chestnuts, pie, and cranberries at the appropriate times as you recite the poem.

CRAFT

Miniature Turkey

Before the program, paint small Styrofoam balls brown. Let the children insert small craft feathers into the balls. Red pipe cleaners will serve for the neck and head. Give children a pipe cleaner to form into a head, and suggest they glue on a small construction paper beak. A few short pieces of pipe cleaner inserted into the bottom of the turkey will keep it from rolling.

Supplies

small Styrofoam balls
construction paper
pipe cleaners
craft feathers
glue

Wrap It Up!

PUBLICITY

Preschoolers and parents or caregivers, come celebrate the joy of the holi-
day season at the _____ Library on
_____. We will have stories, songs, and a festive craft activity.
Call _____ to register.

BOOK SUGGESTIONS

Bunting, Eve. *Night Tree.*

Chocolate, Deborah M. Newton. *My First Kwanzaa Book.*

Hill, Eric. *Spot's First Christmas.*

Moorman, Margaret. *Light the Lights! A Story about Celebrating Hanukkah and Christmas.*

Schotter, Roni. *Hanukkah!*

Stock, Catherine. *Christmas Time.*

Wells, Rosemary. *Max's Christmas.*

FINGER PLAYS

Santa in the Chimney

Here is the chimney,
(hold up fist)
And here is the top,
(cover fist with other hand)
Open the lid,
(remove hand)
And out Santa will pop!
(pop up thumb)

Santa and His Sleigh

Here is old Santa.
(hold up thumb)
Here is his sleigh.
(hold up other thumb)
These are the reindeer
(hold up eight fingers)
Which he drives away.
Dasher, Dancer, Prancer, Vixen,
(bob a finger for each name)
Comet, Cupid, Donner, Blitzen.
Ho, ho, ho,
Away they all go!
*(lock thumbs and run fingers in
front and away)*

Light a Candle on the Kinara

Light a candle on the kinara,
(hold up one finger and touch it)
See how it glows.
Now there are six left to light,
(hold up six fingers)
All sitting in a row.

(repeat with 5, 4, 3, 2, and 1)

The candles are lit on the kinara,
(hold up seven fingers)
See how they glow.
The seven days of Kwanzaa,
All sitting in a row.

Eight Little Candles

Eight little candles,
(hold up eight fingers)
Sitting on the menorah.
One jumped off and danced the
    hora.
Seven . . .
Six . . .
Five . . .
Four . . .
Three . . .
Two . . .
One . . .

SONGS

Hanukkah Song

  Dm
Oh, Hanukkah, Oh, Hanukkah,

    A7   Dm
Come light the menorah. Let's have a party,

    A7   Dm
We'll all dance the hora. Gather round the table,

    A7   Dm Gm
We'll give you a treat. Shining tops to play with,

    A7   Dm   Dm
And pancakes to eat. And while we are dancing,

        A7   Dm
The candles are burning low.

      A7   Dm
One for each night, they will shed a

 A7   Dm
Sweet light, to remind us of

 Gm   A7
Days long ago.

      Dm
Days long ago.

We Wish You a Merry Christmas

    F   Bb
We wish you a merry Christmas,

  G7   C
We wish you a merry Christmas,

  A7   Dm
We wish you a merry Christmas,

   Gm C7 F
And a happy New Year!

    F   Bb
Now bring us a figgy pudding,

  G7   C
Now bring us a figgy pudding,

  A7   Dm
Now bring us a figgy pudding,

   Gm C7 F
And bring it out here.

    F   Bb
We won't go until we get some,

  G7   C
We won't go until we get some,

  A7   Dm
We won't go until we get some,

   Gm C7 F
So bring it out here.

(repeat first verse)

FLANNEL BOARD POEM

The Toy Shop

Here is the toy shop,
And happy are we
For there are so many, many
Toys here to see.

Wonderful toys
All in a row,
And bright colored tops
That sing as they go.

And here in a box
Is a doll that can talk.
And here is a soft wooly dog
That can walk.

Just see this funny old
Jack in the box.
Watch him pop out.
Oh my, what a shock!

Here is the counter
Piled high with the toys,
For you little girls
And you little boys.

We hope, wonderful toys,
That some of you may
Come straight to us
On Christmas Day.

Directions

Enlarge the patterns on a photocopier and make the story figures out of felt. For tips on making flannel board figures see the section on flannel board storytelling in the introduction.

CRAFT

Wrapping Paper

Before the program, cut pieces of sponge into festive shapes. Give each child a large sheet of butcher paper and let him or her dip the sponge into washable tempera paint to make prints on the paper. Potatoes will also make very good prints. You could also carve holiday designs into several potatoes before you do the program.

Supplies

washable paint
potatoes
sponges
paper

PART TWO

MULTICULTURAL PROGRAMS

Native American Tales

PUBLICITY

Enjoy Native American stories, songs, and activities at the
_____ Library on _____. Make a Chippewa dream
catcher to take home. Call _____ to register. Preschoolers,
ages 3–6.

BOOK SUGGESTIONS

Ata, Te. *Baby Rattlesnake.*

Bruchac, Joseph. *The First Strawberries.*

Gates, Frieda. *Owl Eyes.*

Grossman, Virginia. *Ten Little Rabbits.*

Steptoe, John. *The Story of Jumping Mouse: A Native American Legend.*

Stevens, Janet. *Coyote Steals the Blanket: A Ute Tale.*

Swamp, Chief Jake. *Giving Thanks: A Native American Good Morning Message.*

Troughton, Joanna. *How the Birds Changed Their Feathers: A South American Indian Folk Tale.*

FINGER PLAYS

Touch the Earth

Feel the warmth of the morning sun,
    (encircle arms overhead)
And touch the new sweet earth.
    (touch the ground)
Listen to the whispering wind,
    (cup hand around ear)
And let your heart be filled with joy.
    (put hands on heart)

Mother Earth

Mother Earth gives us so many things,
    (trace the shape of the Earth in
     the air)
Flowers that bloom,
    (cup hands and move arms up)
And birds that sing,
    (interlock thumbs and flap fingers)
The beautiful mountains,
    (indicate mountain shapes with
     hands)
Lakes and rivers so blue,
    (make wavy motions with hands)
We must protect these gifts,
Both me and you.
    (point to self and children)

FLANNEL BOARD STORY

How Grandmother Spider Stole the Sun

This Muskogee (Creek) tale can be found on page 49 in *Keepers of the Earth* by Michael J. Caduto. Enlarge the story figures provided on a photocopier. Make the figures with felt and use a piece of white hair net for the spider's web. For tips on making story figures see the section on flannel board storytelling in the introduction.

VIDEO

Show *The Owl Who Married a Goose* from Celebrity Films (8 minutes).

CRAFT

Dream Catcher

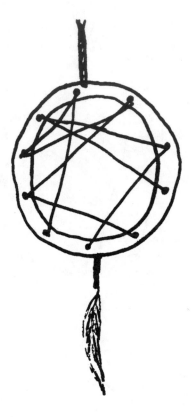

Prior to the program, cut rings out of poster board or paper plates and punch holes around the ring. Give the children yarn to weave through the ring. (Wrap tape around the ends of the yarn to make it easy for them to thread through the holes.) Help them tie a feather to the bottom. Explain to the children that the dream catcher will catch bad dreams, but good dreams will float through the web and slip down the feather onto a sleeping person. Suggest that they hang the dream catcher over their beds.

Supplies

poster board or paper plates
craft feathers
yarn

Hawaiian Island Adventure

PUBLICITY

Get away from it all at the _____ Library on
_____, and join us on an island adventure. Listen to
stories, make a lei and grass skirt, and listen to some Hawaiian tunes as
you dance the hula. Call _____ to register. Preschoolers,
ages 3–6.

BOOK SUGGESTIONS

Feeney, Stephanie. *Hawaii Is a Rainbow*.

MacDonald, Golden. *The Little Island*.

Mellor, Corrine. *Clark the Toothless Shark*.

Robbins, Ken. *Beach Days*.

Seymour, Peter. *What's at the Beach?*

ACTION RHYMES

I Am a Volcano

I am a volcano.
> *(squat down with hands around knees)*

Hear me rumble.
> *(tremble and rumble)*

The lava deep down in me,
Is beginning to bubble.
Something is going to happen,
Happen very soon!
I'm erupting with a
Big gigantic BOOM!!!
> *(jump up and extend arms upward)*

Leis

Garlands of beautiful flowers,
Around our necks we wear,
> *(pretend to put on a lei)*

We give our leis to friends,
> *(pretend to put a lei on someone)*

To show them that we care.

CRAFTS

Paper Leis

Give each child a piece of thread with a poster board "needle" taped to one end. Supply the children with small squares of tissue paper that have holes poked in them. Let the children make the leis. Help them tie the leis when they finish.

"Grass" Skirts

Fasten crepe paper strips to a piece of yarn and tie around the child's waist. Parent helpers may be needed for this activity.

ACTIVITY

Hula Dance

Play Hawaiian music after the children have completed their crafts. You should have no trouble getting the children to dance the hula once they get their grass skirts on.

Tales from China

PUBLICITY

Enjoy listening to stories and folk tales from China at the _____

_____ Library on _____. We will also see a

short video and make a dragon puppet. Call _____ to

register. Preschoolers, ages 3–6.

BOOK SUGGESTIONS

Cheng, Hou-Tien. *The Six Chinese Brothers.*

Demi. *Dragon Kites and Dragonflies: A Collection of Chinese Nursery Rhymes.*

Mosel, Arlene. *Tikki, Tikki, Tembo.*

Wolkstein, Diane. *The Magic Wings: A Tale from China.*

FINGER PLAYS

Several of the rhymes in Demi's *Dragon Kites and Dragonflies: A Collection of Chinese Nursery Rhymes* can be done as finger plays.

FLANNEL BOARD STORY

Two of Everything

The Chinese folk tale "Two of Everything" can be found in *The Arbuthnot Anthology of Children's Literature* by May Hill Arbuthnot on pages 333–4. You will need to make two identical story figures with each pattern provided except the pot. Enlarge the patterns on a photocopier. For tips on making story figures see the section on flannel board storytelling in the introduction.

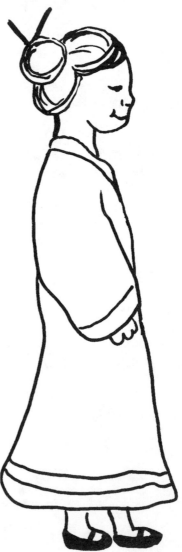

VIDEO

"The Five Chinese Brothers" can be found on the video *The Mysterious Tadpole and Other Stories* from Children's Circle (10 minutes).

CRAFT

Dragon Puppet

Let the children create paper bag dragon puppets by gluing on precut eyes, tongues, fins, fangs, and claws made from red, black, and yellow construction paper.

Supplies

red, black, and yellow construction
    paper
washable markers
glue
paper bags

Russian Snow Fest

PUBLICITY

Russian winters are cold! But we'll warm your heart with some stories

and songs at the _____ Library on

_____. We will also have time for a short video and a craft

activity. Call _____ to register. Preschoolers, ages 3-6.

BOOK SUGGESTIONS

Brett, Jan. *The Mitten*.

Brown, Margaret Wise. *Animals in the Snow*.

Butterworth, Nick. *One Snowy Night*.

Chapman, Cheryl. *Snow on Snow on Snow*.

Croll, Carolyn. *The Little Snowgirl*.

Rockwell, Anne. *First Snowfall*.

ACTION RHYME

The Snowman

Roll him and roll him until he is big,
> *(rolling motion)*

Roll him until he is fat as a pig.
> *(hold out arms to indicate roundness)*

He has two eyes and a hat on his head,
> *(fingers circle eyes, set imaginary hat on head)*

He'll stand there all night,

While we go to bed.
> *(place head on hands, close eyes)*

FINGER PLAY

Snowflakes

Snowflakes falling down, down, down.
> *(flutter fingers downward)*

Gently covering all the town.
> *(move hands to indicate ground)*

Swirling, twirling, down they come.
> *(swirl hands downward)*

One landed on my tongue.
> *(stick out tongue)*

SONG

Wintertime

(*Tune:* "Twinkle, Twinkle, Little Star")

     D   G   D
Snowflakes falling everywhere,

A7   D   A7   D
Old Jack Frost is in the air.

     D   A7   D   A7
Through the silver powdered snow

     D   A7   D   A
Troika, troika, here we go.

    D   D7   G   B7
Hear the sleigh bells ring and chime,

    Em   D   A7   D
There's nothing quite like wintertime.

FINGER PUPPETS

The Mitten

Tell the Russian folk tale, "The Mitten" with finger puppets and a felt mitten that has a hidden Velcro seam. Two sources for the story are *The Mitten* by Jan Brett and *The Mitten* by Alvin Tresselt.

Directions

Use the patterns to create felt animals. Cut the fingers off an old glove and glue the animals to the fingers. Enlarge the mitten pattern on a photocopier and cut the front and back pieces out of felt. Close the seam with the Velcro strips. Decorate the glove with small beads or sequins if desired.

Wear the glove fingers with the puppets attached. As you tell the story, slide each puppet (and glove finger) off your finger when you put that finger in the mitten. At the end of the story, when the mouse squeezes in, rip the Velcro seam open and let all the animals pop out.

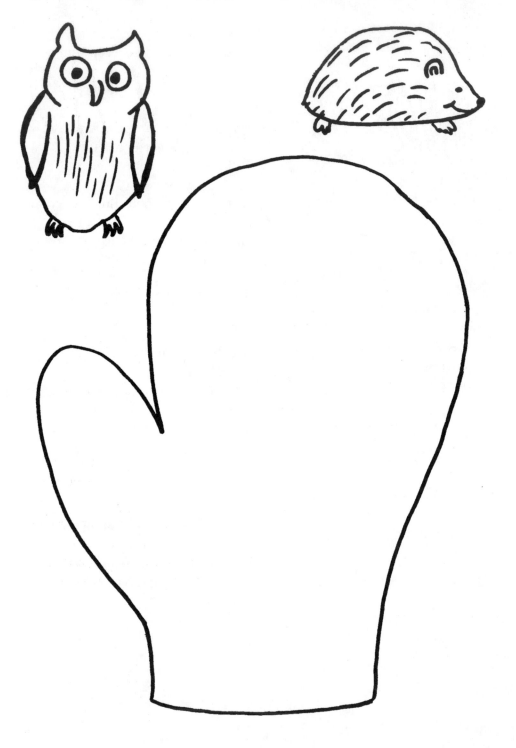

POEM

Old Jack Frost

Who gives the tree its new fall suit?
Old Jack Frost.

Who sweetens up the ripened fruit?
Who makes the birds fly a warmer
    route?
    *(pause and let the children join
    in when you repeat the refrain:
    "Old Jack Frost")*
Old Jack Frost.

Who brings the walnut tumbling
    down?
Who makes the chestnut sweet and
    brown?
Who yellows up the pumpkin's
    gown?
Old Jack Frost.

Who makes the lace-designed
    windows?
Old Jack Frost.

Who nips the tip of your chilly nose?
Who bites even at bundled-up toes?
Old Jack Frost.

Who makes the white snow pile up
    deep?
Who makes you crawl up in a heap
And call for covers when you sleep?
Old Jack Frost.

VIDEO

Show *Matrioska* from Contemporary Films (5 minutes).

CRAFT

Grandfather Frost

Let the children glue precut construction paper pieces to a toilet paper tube to create a Grandfather Frost figure. Use light blue construction paper for his coat and hat. Provide cotton or fiberfill stuffing for his beard and the trim on his coat and hat. Let them sprinkle their figures with silver glitter.

Supplies

light blue construction paper
cotton or fiberfill
toilet paper tubes
silver glitter
glue

African Tales

PUBLICITY

Delight in stories and folk tales from Africa at the _____

_____ Library on _____. We will also have time for a

short video and a craft activity. Call _____ to register.

Preschoolers, ages 3–6.

BOOK SUGGESTIONS

Aardema, Verna. *Why Mosquitoes Buzz in People's Ears.*

Dayrell, Elphinstone. *Why the Sun and the Moon Live in the Sky.*

Gray, Nigel. *A Country Far Away.*

Grifalconi, Ann. *The Village of Round and Square Houses.*

Isadora, Rachel. *At the Crossroads.*

Kimmel, Eric. *Anansi and the Moss-Covered Rock.*

McDermott, Gerald. *Zomo the Rabbit: A Trickster Tale from West Africa.*

ACTION RHYME

Lion Hunt

I'm going on a lion hunt.
I'm going on a lion hunt.
    (slap thighs alternately)
I see a swamp.
    (shade eyes with hands)
Can't go under it,
Can't go over it,
    (slap thighs)
Have to go through it.
Slush, slush, slush, slush.
    (rub hands together)

I'm going on a lion hunt.
I'm going on a lion hunt.
    (slap thighs)
I see a bridge.
    (shade eyes with hands)
Can't go under it,
Can't go through it,
    (slap thighs)
Have to go over it.
Thump, thump, thump, thump.
    (stamp feet)

I'm going on a lion hunt.
I'm going on a lion hunt.
    (slap thighs)
I see a stream.
    (shade eyes with hands)
Can't go under it,
Can't go over it,
    (slap thighs)
Have to go through it.
Splash, splash, splash, splash.
    (do swim strokes)

I'm going on a lion hunt.
I'm going on a lion hunt.
    (slap thighs)
I see a tree.
    (shade eyes with hand)
Let's go see.
    (slap thighs)
Up, up, up, up.
    (climbing motion)

I see a cave.
    (shade eyes with hand)
Down, down, down, down.
    (climbing down motion)
Let's go see.
    (slap thighs)

I feel something.
    (feel with hands)
I feel something furry.
It feels like a lion.
It looks like a lion.
It IS a lion!
    (quickly slap thighs)

Up.
    (climb up)
Down.
    (climb down)
Splash, splash, splash.
    (swim strokes)
Thump, thump, thump.
    (stamp feet)
Slush, slush, slush.
    (rub hands together)
Woo!
    (collapse)
I'm not going on a lion hunt again!

FINGER PLAY

Five Little Monkeys

Five little monkeys swinging in a
tree,
(hold up five fingers)
Teasing Mr. Crocodile: "You can't
catch me!"
(wag finger)
Along comes crocodile quiet as
can be,
*(place palms together to indicate
jaws, make wavy motion)*
And, SNAP!
(snap palms together)
Four little monkeys swinging in a
tree . . .
(hold up four fingers)

(repeat with 3, 2, and 1)

SNAP! Ha, ha, you missed me!

FLANNEL BOARD STORY

Spider and the Magic Stone

Tell the story "Spider and the Magic
Stone," using the story figures that
follow. This story can be found in
*Spiders, Crabs, and Creepy Crawlers:
Two African Folktales* by Kathleen
Arnott.

Enlarge the patterns on a photocopier to the size appropriate for
your flannel board. For tips on making story figures, check the section
on flannel board storytelling in the
introduction.

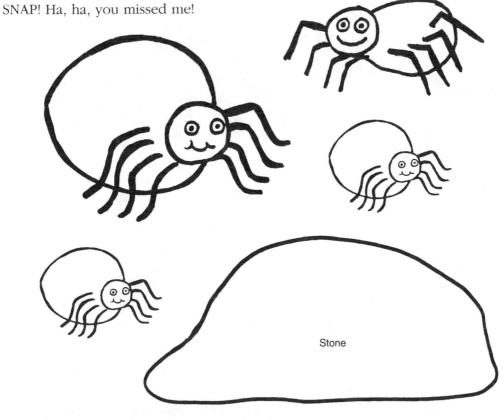

Stone

VIDEO

Show *Mufaro's Beautiful Daughters* from Weston Woods (14 minutes).

CRAFT

African Mask

Precut mask shapes from poster board (any color). Let the children glue on craft feathers, glitter, and any other decorative materials you have on hand. Help them glue a craft stick to the bottom of the mask.

Supplies

poster board
craft feathers
washable markers
glue

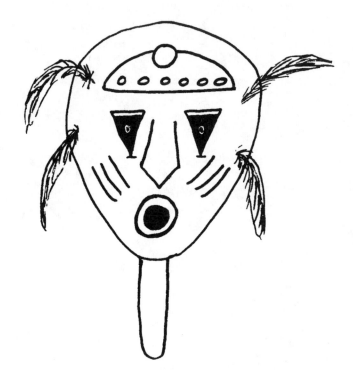

A Mexican Fiesta

PUBLICITY

Join us for a Mexican fiesta at the _____ Library on _____. Hear tales from Mexico, do a hat dance, enjoy our festive refreshments, and make your own maracas to take home. Call _____ to register. Preschoolers, ages 3–6.

BOOK SUGGESTIONS

Aardema, Verna. *Borreguita and the Coyote.*

Dupré, Judith. *The Mouse Bride: A Mayan Folk Tale.*

Johnston, Tony. *The Tale of Rabbit and Coyote.*

FLANNEL BOARD STORY

The Ant, the Lamb, the Cricket, and the Mouse

This Mexican tale can be found in *The Boy Who Could Do Anything & Other Mexican Folk Tales* by Anita Brenner on pages 19–20. Tell the story using flannel board figures. Enlarge the figures on a photocopier to a size appropriate for your flannel board. For tips on making story figures see the section on flannel board storytelling in the introduction.

ACTIVITY

Mexican Hat Dance

Find a recording of "La Raspa" (the Mexican hat dance song) to play while the children dance around a sombrero you've placed on the floor. Let them shake their maracas (see the craft activity) in time to the music. If your group is large, use several sombreros.

Festive Refreshments

Serve cheese nachos and guacamole with taco chips and fruit punch.

VIDEO

Show *Pedro* from Walt Disney (8 minutes).

CRAFT

Maracas

Before the program, put a few dried beans in a paper cup and place another paper cup over the top. Tape the rims together. Let the children decorate the cups with markers. They can glue thin strips of crepe paper on the ends for a tassel.

Supplies

dried beans
paper cups
tape
washable markers
glue
crepe paper

PART THREE

ANIMALS

Stuffed Animal Pet Show

PUBLICITY

Bring your favorite stuffed-animal pet to the _____
Library on _____. Listen to pet tales, sing pet songs, and
enjoy tasty snacks. Each pet will receive a special prize. Please call
_____ to register. Preschoolers, ages 3–6.

BOOK SUGGESTIONS

Brown, Ruth. *Copycat.*
Crawford, Ron. *Pet?*
Halpern, Shari. *I Have a Pet!*
Keats, Ezra Jack. *Pet Show!*
Lee, Hector Viveros. *I Had a Hippopotamus.*

Luttrell, Ida. *Mattie's Little Possum Pet.*
Seymour, Tres. *I Love My Buzzard.*

71

ACTION RHYME

Pets

Hop, hop, hop like your bunny.
    (suit actions to words)
Run, run, run like your dog.
Walk, walk, walk like your cat.
Jump, jump, jump like your frog.
Swim, swim, swim like your
    goldfish.
Fly, fly, fly like your bird.
Then sit right down and don't say a
    word.

FINGER PLAY

This Is My Turtle

This is my turtle.
    *(make a fist with thumb
    extended)*
He lives in a shell.
    (hide thumb in fist)
He likes his home very well.
    (nod head)
He pokes his head out
    (pop out thumb)
When he wants to eat,
    (wiggle thumb)
And pulls it back in
    (hide thumb)
When he wants to sleep.

SONG

Rags

I've got a dog, his name is Rags.
He eats so much that his tummy
    sags.
His ears flip flop and his tail wig
    wags,
And when he walks, he walks zig
    zag.

Chorus
    He goes flip flop, wig wag,
        zig zag.
    (repeat this line three times)

I love Rags and he loves me.
My dog Rags he likes to play,
He rolls himself in the mud all day.
When I call he won't obey,
He always walks the other way.

    (repeat chorus)

FINGER PUPPETS

This Kitty

This kitty said, "I smell a mouse,"
This kitty said, "Let's hunt through
    the house."
This kitty said, "Let's go creepity
    creep."
This kitty said, "Is the mouse
    asleep?"
And the little mouse said, "Squeakity
    squeak,"
And ran in his hole and stayed for a
    week.

Directions

Use the patterns to make four kittens and one mouse out of poster board or felt. Attach Velcro to the back of each puppet and to the fingers of a glove. Put the mouse puppet on your thumb. On the last line of the poem tuck your thumb out of sight.

ACTIVITY

Pet Show

Ask the children to bring their stuffed-animal pets to a designated table to register for the pet show. Then display the pets on a table. Serve children snacks while you write complimentary or funny descriptions of each pet on the prize ribbons (see illustration).

As the prize ribbons are awarded, have each child come and get his or her pet. Announce the pet owner's name and read the words on the ribbon. Place the ribbon on the pet. Applaud after each prize is presented.

VIDEO

Show *House Cats* from Phoenix (15 minutes).

Fabulous Frogs

PUBLICITY

Preschoolers and their parents or caregivers are invited to join us at the
_____ Library on _____ for a celebration of
our amphibian friends. We will have frog stories, frog games, frog songs, a
short video, and a craft activity. Call _____ to register.

BOOK SUGGESTIONS

Arnold, Tedd. *Green Wilma*.

Kalan, Robert. *Jump, Frog, Jump*.

Kent, Jack. *The Caterpillar and the Polliwog*.

London, Jonathan. *Froggy Learns to Swim*.

Mann, Pamela. *The Frog Princess*.

Schneider, Rex. *Wide-Mouthed Frog*.

FINGER PLAYS

Frog's Song

I am a little frog,
Hopping on a log.
*(hop fingers on palm of other
hand)*
Listen to my song.
(make frog sounds)
I sleep all winter long.
(place head on hands)
I wake up and peek out,
Up I jump, all about.
(hop fingers on palm)
I catch flies,
(move tongue in and out)
I wink my eyes.
(wink eyes)
I hop and hop,
(stand and hop)
And then I stop.

Grandad Frog

Grandad Frog sat down on a stone,
*(make a fist with thumb pointing
up)*
Croaking a song as he sat there alone.
*(move thumb and make frog
sounds)*
Along came a boy with a fishing net,
(walk two fingers of other hand)
And Grandad Frog said, "It's time to
get wet."
Ker-plunk! Splash!
*(dive thumb downward and do
swimming motions with arms)*
Grandad Frog got away that day.
The boy couldn't catch him,
Not today, anyway!
*(shake head and shrug
shoulders)*

GAME

Leap Frog

Children really get into this activity,
and it releases a lot of energy. Frog
sound effects make it fun too. With
an assistant, demonstrate how to
play leap frog. Group the children in
threes or fours, and let each group
have a turn leaping across the room.

SONG WITH VISUAL ENHANCEMENT

Five Little Frogs

Five green and speckled frogs,
Sat on a speckled log,
Eating some most delicious bugs.
Yum! Yum!
One jumped into the pool,
Where it was nice and cool,
Then there were four green speckled
frogs.
Glub, glub.

(repeat with 4, 3, 2, *and* 1)

No green speckled frogs.

Directions

Cover a wrapping paper tube with light brown construction paper or paint. Draw or paint spots on the tube. Staple the frogs to thin poster board loops and slip them onto the tube. When you sing the song, hold the tube horizontally and flip each frog down at the appropriate time in the song.

VIDEO

You may want to show a short segment of *Frog and Toad Together* from Churchill (30 minutes). It contains the same chapters as Lobel's book of the same title.

CRAFT

Egg-Carton Frog

Before the program, cut out a section of an egg carton for each frog body, one per child. Let children add small pom-poms for eyes and glue on construction paper legs. They can then glue the frog onto a construction paper lily pad.

Supplies

construction paper
egg carton
pom-poms
washable markers
glue

Dog Days

PUBLICITY

Do you love dogs? Join us in a celebration of our "K9" friends at the

_____ Library on _____. We'll have dog

stories, songs, poems, and a puppy puppet craft. Call _____

to register. Preschoolers, ages 3–6.

BOOK SUGGESTIONS

Bryant, Donna. *My Dog Jessie.*

Crawford, Ron. *Pet?*

Evans, Katie. *Hunky Dory Ate It.*

Hall, Donald. *I Am the Dog, I Am the Cat.*

Hill, Eric. *Where's Spot?*

Inkpen, Mick. *Kipper.*

Kopper, Lisa. *Daisy Thinks She Is a Baby.*

Martin, David. *Lizzie and Her Puppy.*

FINGER PLAY

Bowser

This is Bowser's dog house, and
  (hands form point)
This is Bowser's bed.
  (smooth covers)
This is the pan that holds his milk
  (form bowl with hands)
And other good things he's fed.

This is the collar that goes around
  his neck
  (make circle with hands)
With *Bowser* in letters new.
Take a stick and throw it,
  (throw stick)
And he'll bring it back to you.
  (pat head)
Good dog, Bowser!

FLANNEL BOARD POEM

Old Mother Hubbard

Old Mother Hubbard
Went to the cupboard,
To get her poor dog a bone;
But when she got there
The cupboard was bare,
And so the poor dog had none.

She took a clean dish
To get him some tripe;
But when she came back
He was smoking a pipe.

She went to the fruiterer's
To buy him some fruit;
But when she came back
He was playing a flute.

She went to the hatter's
To buy him a hat;
But when she came back
He was feeding the cat.

She went to the barber's
To buy him a wig;
But when she came back
He was dancing a jig.

wig

She went to the tailor's
To buy him a coat;
But when she came back
He was riding a goat.

She went to the cobbler's
To buy him some shoes;
But when she came back
He was reading the news.

She went to the hosier's
To buy him some hose;
But when she came back
He was dressed in his clothes.

The dame made a curtsey,
The dog made a bow;
The dame said, "Your servant,"
The dog said, "Bow-wow."

—Mother Goose

Directions

Enlarge the patterns on a photo-copier to the desired size for your flannel board. Make the story figures out of felt. (See the section on flan-nel board storytelling in the intro-duction for tips on making story figures.) Place each item on your flannel board at the appropriate time in the poem. Add the various accessories to the dog as you recite the poem.

SONG

Bingo

```
      G          C       D
There was a farmer had a dog
      G       D       G
And Bingo was his name-o.
Em Am     D   G     C   Am
B-I-N-G-O, B-I-N-G-O, B-I-N-G-O,
      D7              C   G
And Bingo was his name-o.
```

VIDEO

Show *Harry the Dirty Dog* from Barr Films (15 minutes).

CRAFT

Puppy Puppet

Let the children create simple paper bag puppets by gluing on precut construction paper ears, tongues, and tails; pom-pom noses; and craft eyes. They can also use crayons or markers for details.

Supplies

construction paper
googly eyes
paper bags
pom-poms
crayons
glue

Meow!

PUBLICITY

Do you love cats? Come to the _____ Library on
_____ for some feline fun. We'll have stories, songs, and a short
video. Enjoy creating a cat mask to take home. Please call _____
to register. Preschoolers, ages 3–6.

BOOK SUGGESTIONS

Allen, Pamela. *My Cat Maisey.*

Aatley, Judy. *When One Cat Woke Up.*

Dunbar, Joyce. *Four Fierce Kittens.*

Hersom, Kathleen. *The Copy Cat.*

Leman, Martin. *Ten Cats and Their Tales.*

Slavin, Bill. *The Cat Came Back.*

Ward, Cindy. *Cookie's Week.*

FINGER PLAYS

The Cat and the Mice

The cat is asleep, she can't hear a
  sound.
  (place head on hands)
The mice can come out and run
  around.
  (skitter fingers around like mice)
Skittery—skattery, skittery—skattery,
Skittery—skattery, skittery—skattery.

The cat is awake, she hears the mice
  play,
  *(open eyes wide and cup ear
  with hand)*
But the mice perk their ears, they
  hear the cat say,
MEOW!

The mice ran away, to hide in their
  holes,
So the cat can't reach them with her
  paws.
  (make clawing action)
Skittery—skattery, skittery—skattery,
  *(skitter fingers around and
  behind back)*
Skittery—skattery, skittery—skattery.

The mice are hidden away very
  deep,
So the cat stretches out,
And goes back to sleep.
Meow.
  *(stretch and place head on
  hands)*

Two Little Cats

Two little kitty cats,
  (hold up two fingers)
Lying fast asleep,
  (put head on hands)
Soft and fluffy,
All in a heap.
Along came a puppy dog,
Playing near,
"Bark, Bark, Bark,"
He said right in their ear.
  (cover ears)
One little puppy
  (hold up one finger)
Being chased by the two cats—
  (hold up two fingers)
Did you ever play tag like that?

SONG

Five Kittens in the Bed

(Tune: "Ten in the Bed")

There were five kittens in the bed,
And the little one said,
"Roll over, I'm crowded."
So they all rolled over, and one fell
  out;

There were four kittens in the bed . . .

  (repeat with 3, 2, and 1)

And the little one said,
"I'm lonely."

So they all got back in bed,
And the little one said,
"Good Night!"

FLANNEL BOARD POEM

The Owl and the Pussy Cat

There are many picture books, such as *The Owl and the Pussy Cat* by Jan Brett, and poetry collections that feature this well-known poem by Edward Lear. Obtain a copy of the poem and present it on the flannel board using the patterns provided.

Enlarge the story figures on a photocopier to a size appropriate for your flannel board. For tips on making story figures see the section on flannel board storytelling in the introduction.

S. S. Sweet Pea

HONEY

moon

CREATIVE DRAMATICS

The Three Little Kittens

Read "The Three Little Kittens" by Paul Galdone or another picture book version of this poem that you have on hand. After reading the book, choose a child to be the mother cat and three others to play the parts of the kittens. If you have a group of twenty or less, you may want to include all the children. Reread the poem and encourage the children to perform the actions (looking for mittens, washing mittens, eating pie, etc.).

VIDEO

Show *Let's Give Kitty a Bath* from Phoenix Films (12 minutes).

CRAFT

Cat Mask

Before the program, cut eye holes in paper plates and attach craft sticks. Let the children color the masks with markers and glue on yarn whiskers, pink pom-pom noses, and precut construction paper ears.

Supplies

construction paper
washable markers
pink pom-poms
craft sticks
paper plates
yarn

Flap
Your Wings

PUBLICITY

Join us at the _____ Library on _____
for stories, songs, and rhymes about our feathered friends. Create your
own wings with real feathers. Call _____ to register.
Preschoolers, ages 3–6.

BOOK SUGGESTIONS

Ehlert, Lois. *Feathers for Lunch*.

Kasza, Keiko. *A Mother for Choco*.

Kent, Jack. *Round Robin*.

Kleven, Elisa. *The Lion and the Little Red Bird*.

Silverman, Erica. *Don't Fidget a Feather*.

Tafuri, Nancy. *Have You Seen My Duckling?*

Van Laan, Nancy. *The Big Fat Worm*.

Waddell, Martin. *Owl Babies*.

FINGER PLAYS

The Green Leafy Tree

We went to the meadow and what
   did we see?
A green leafy tree.
   (hold arms up, elbows bent,
      spread fingers)
We went to the meadow and what
   did we see?
A nest in the tree, the green leafy
   tree.
   (cup hands, hold arms up)
We went to the meadow and what
   did we see?
Oh! Speckled blue eggs in the nest;
   (touch thumbs to index fingers,
      cup hands)
In the tree, the green leafy tree.
   (hold arms up)
We went to the meadow and what
   did we see?
Oh! Two baby birds
   (cross wrists and thumbs and
      flap fingers)
From the speckled blue eggs,
   (thumbs touch index fingers)
The eggs in the nest,
   (cup hands)
In the tree, the green leafy tree.
   (hold arms up)

Two Little Blackbirds

Two little blackbirds
   (extend index fingers)
Sitting on a hill.
One named Jack,
   (bob one finger)
One named Jill.
   (bob other finger)
Fly away Jack.
   (put right hand behind back)
Fly away Jill.
   (put left hand behind back)
Come back Jack.
   (bring back right hand, extend
      finger)
Come back Jill.
   (bring back left hand, extend
      finger)
Two little blackbirds
Sitting on a hill.

—Mother Goose

FINGER PUPPETS

Five Little Chickadees

Five little chickadees, pecking at the
    door;
One flew away, and then there were
    four.
Four little chickadees, sitting
    in a tree;
One flew away, and then there
    were three.
Three little chickadees, looking at you;
One flew away, and then there were
    two.
Two little chickadees, sitting in the
    sun;
One flew away, and then there was
    one.
One little chickadee, left all alone;
One flew away, and then there were
    none.
Come back little chickadees!

Directions

Use the pattern to make five chickadees out of felt or poster board.
Attach Velcro to the back of each
bird and to the fingers of a glove.

While you say the rhyme, put
your gloved hand behind your back
each time a chickadee flies away.
Bring your hand back with one
more finger folded down each time.
Bring all the chickadees back at the
end of the rhyme.

SONG WITH STORY TREE

The Green Grass Grew All Around

In the woods there was a tree,
The prettiest tree that you ever did
    see.
Oh, the tree in the woods,

Chorus

> And the green grass grew all
>   around,
> All around,
> And the green grass grew all
>   around.

And in the tree there was a nest,
Oh, prettiest nest you ever did see.
Nest in the tree,
And the tree in the woods,

>   *(repeat chorus after each verse)*

And in that nest there was an egg,
Oh, prettiest egg you ever did see.
Egg in the nest,
Nest in the tree,
And the tree in the woods,

And on that egg there was a bird,
The prettiest bird that you ever did
    see.
Bird on the egg,
Egg in the nest,
Nest in the tree,
And the tree in the woods,

And on that bird there was a feather,
The prettiest feather that you ever
    did see.
Feather on the bird,
Bird on the egg,
Egg in the nest,
Nest in the tree,
And the tree in the woods,

And on that feather there was a flea,
The prettiest flea that you ever did
    see.
Flea on the feather,
Feather on the bird,
Bird on the egg,
Egg in the nest,
Nest in the tree,
And the tree in the woods,

Directions

Cut a tree silhouette out of heavy cardboard (suggested size range from two to five feet). Cut a slot in the bottom of the tree and insert another piece of cardboard. With strong tape, attach the base of the tree to a square of plywood. Cover the top of the tree with green felt and the trunk with brown felt. Use the patterns to make a felt bird, nest, egg, feather, and flea. Place the figures on the story tree as you sing the song.

The story tree may also be used for other rhymes, songs, and stories involving trees such as *Caps for Sale* by Esphyr Slobodkina, *Goodnight Owl* by Pat Hutchins, "Five Little Monkeys" (see "Going Ape" program), and the song "Kookaburra" by Marian Sinclair.

VIDEO

Show *Owl Moon and Other Stories* from Children's Circle (10 minutes).

CRAFT

Wings

Trace wing shapes, large enough to cover most of a child's arm, onto thin poster board or heavy paper.

Tape pipecleaner loops, which would fit over a child's arm, onto the back of the wings. Let the children glue on craft feathers and flap their wings around the room.

Supplies

thin poster board or heavy paper
pipe cleaners
craft feathers
glue

Marvelous Marsupials

PUBLICITY

Preschoolers and parents or caretakers, come join us at the _____ _____ Library on _____ for stories, songs, and finger plays about koalas, kangaroos, wombats, and more. A craft activity will follow. Call _____ to register.

BOOK SUGGESTIONS

Argent, Kerry. *Happy Birthday, Wombat!*

———. *Wombat and Bandicoot: Best of Friends.*

Fox, Mem. *Koala Lou.*

Jensen, Kiersten. *Possum in the House.*

Luttrell, Ida. *Mattie's Little Possum Pet.*

Payne, Emmy. *Katy No-Pocket.*

Trinca, Rod. *One Woolly Wombat.*

Vaughan, Marcia K. *Wombat Stew.*

ACTION RHYMES

The Brown Kangaroo

The brown kangaroo is very funny.
She leaps and runs and hops like a
    bunny.
    (hop around)
And on her stomach is a pocket so
    wide,
    *(place hand on stomach to indi-
    cate pocket)*
Her baby can jump in and go for a
    ride.
    (jump other hand into "pocket")

The Furry Koala

The furry koala is as cute as can be.
She loves to climb in her eucalyptus
    tree.
    (do climbing motion)
Her ears are fluffy and her fur is
    gray,
    (point to ears)
And she nibbles on leaves all
    through the day.
    (pretend to nibble)

SONG

Marvelous Marsupials

(Tune: "Frère Jacques")

  C
Marvelous marsupials
Marvelous marsupials

     G   C
What are they?
     G   C
What are they?

   C
Kangaroos and wallabies,
Bandicoots and possums,

      G   C
Wombats and koalas.
      G   C
Wombats and koalas.

   C
They have pouches
They have pouches

    G   C
For their babies
    G   C
For their babies

   C
Kangaroos and wallabies,
Bandicoots and possums,

      G C
Wombats and koalas.
      G C
Wombats and koalas.

DRAWING STORY

Mystery Marsupial

On the other side of the world there is a big ocean.

And in that ocean there are some islands. Some are large and some are small and the waves crash upon the shores. Here are some waves.

On these islands there are some amazing creatures that cannot be found anywhere else in the world. One of these wonderful animals has furry ears, a charming face, and looks a little like a teddy bear. Do you know what it is?

(Turn drawing right-side up.)

CRAFT

Kangaroos and Joeys

Let the children color pictures of kangaroos and glue on precut pouches. Provide them with paper joeys to insert in the pockets.

Supplies

paper
crayons
glue

Oink!

PUBLICITY

What did the sow say to the hog? "You're such a pig!" Come to the

_____ Library on _____ for a

celebration of our lovable, smart, curly tailed friends. Make an apple pig to

take home or eat! Call _____ to register. Preschoolers, ages

3–6.

BOOK SUGGESTIONS

Boland, Janice. *Annabel*.

Galdone, Paul. *The Three Little Pigs*.

Hutchins, Pat. *Little Pink Pig*.

McPhail, David. *Pig Pig Grows Up*.

Palatini, Margie. *Piggie Pie*.

Pomerantz, Charlotte. *Piggy in the Puddle*.

Rayner, Mary. *Mrs. Pig's Bulk Buy*.

Waddell, Martin. *The Pig in the Pond*.

Wood, Audrey. *Piggies*.

FINGER PLAYS

Two Mother Pigs

Two mother pigs lived in a pen.
(show thumbs)
Each had four babies, and that made
ten.
(show fingers and thumb)
These four babies were soft and
pink.
*(hold up one hand, four fingers
up)*
These four babies were black as ink.
*(hold up other hand, four fingers
up)*
All eight babies loved to play.
And they rolled, and they rolled, in
the mud all day.
(roll hands over each other)
At night with their mothers, they
curled up in a heap,
And squealed and squealed until
they went to sleep.
(make fists palms up)

The Pigs

Piggie Wig and Piggie Wee,
  *(Hold up hands with palms
  facing body and fingertips
  touching. This is the gate.
  Hold up a thumb to indicate
  each piggie.)*
Hungry pigs as pigs could be,
For their dinner had to wait
Down behind the barnyard gate.
  (hide thumbs behind "gate")

Piggie Wig and Piggie Wee
Climbed the barnyard gate to see.
Peeping through the gate so high,
  *(insert thumbs through index
  and middle fingers that form
  the "gate")*
But no dinner could they spy.

Piggie Wig and Piggie Wee
Got down sad as pigs could be;
But the gate soon opened wide,
  (open hands)
And they scampered forth outside.
  ("scamper" thumbs forward)

Piggie Wig and Piggie Wee,
What was their delight to see
Dinner ready, not far off—
Such a full and tempting trough!
  (cup hands to form trough)

Piggie Wig and Piggie Wee,
Greedy pigs as pigs could be,
For their dinner ran pell-mell,
In the trough both piggies fell.
  (plop thumbs into cupped hands)

—Emilie Poulsson

FLANNEL BOARD STORY

Tell the story of the "Three Little Pigs" (see the Paul Galdone book, for example) using the story figures. Enlarge the patterns on a photocopy machine to the appropriate size for your flannel board. Use felt to make the figures and houses. Cut the windows out of the houses so when you place them over the pigs on the flannel board, you can see the pigs inside.

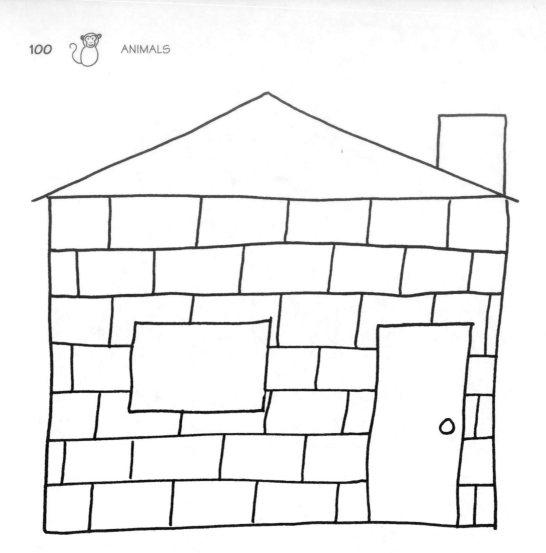

VIDEO

Show *The Pigs Wedding* from Weston Woods (7 minutes).

CRAFT

Apple Pigs

To prepare for this craft, cut the appropriate number of apples in half (horizontally, not lengthwise). You'll need a whole apple and a half apple for each child. With the help of the parents or caregivers, the children will use the toothpicks to attach the head (apple half) to the body (the whole apple). Position the whole apple so the stem becomes the pig's tail. Insert four toothpicks for legs. Have children use their (clean) thumbnails to press in raisins for eyes and tear up two flaps of apple skin for ears. Minature marshmallows can be pressed onto the apple stem or the end of a toothpick for the pig's nose.

Supplies

1¹/₂ apples per child
toothpicks
raisins
miniature marshmallows

Just Ducky

PUBLICITY

Join us at the _____ Library on _____
for a celebration of adorable webbed-footed creatures. Listen to stories
and sing songs. Make your own webbed feet and duck bill. Then waddle and
quack to your heart's content. Call _____ to register.
Preschoolers, ages 3–6.

BOOK SUGGESTIONS

Brown, Margaret Wise. *The Golden Egg Book.*

Casey, Patricia. *Quack, Quack.*

Ginsburg, Mirra. *Across the Stream.*

Otto, Carolyn. *Ducks, Ducks, Ducks.*

Primavera, Elise. *The Three Dots.*

Raffi. *Five Little Ducks.*

Waddell, Martin. *Farmer Duck.*

Whybrow, Ian. *Quacky Quack-Quack!*

FINGER PLAY

Little Yellow Duck

I'm a little yellow duck,
  *(make quacking motion with
  hand)*
Who loves to see the rain.
  *(wiggle fingers downward to
  indicate rain)*
A little yellow duck, now I will
  explain.
  *(make quacking motion with
  hand)*
I love to see the rain come down,
  (wiggle fingers to indicate rain)
Then I can swim all over the town.
  (make paddling motions)
I'm a little yellow duck,
  (quacking motion)
Who loves to see the rain.
  (wiggle fingers to indicate rain)
Splash, splash, splash!

ACTION RHYME

Funny Duck

Waddle, waddle, waddle duck,
  (squat and waddle)
Waddle to the pond.
Paddle, paddle, paddle duck,
Paddle round and round.
  (paddle with hands)
Tail up, head down, funny little
  duck,
Tail up, head down, funny little
  duck.
  *(Place hands behind back to
  represent tail. Move head
  downward.)*

FINGER PUPPETS

Five Little Ducks

Five little ducks went out one day
Over the hills and far away.
Mother duck said, "Quack, quack,
  quack, quack!"
But only four little ducks came back.

  (repeat with 4, 3, 2, 1, *and* none)

Sad mother duck went out one day
Over the hills and far away.
Mother duck said, "Quack, quack,
  quack, quack,"
And all of the five little ducks came
  back!

Directions

Use the pattern to make five ducks out of felt or poster board. Attach Velcro to the back of each duck and to the fingers of a glove. The Velcro should be attached on the fingernail side of the glove (not palm side) because you will be folding your fingers down, to hide the ducks. If you prefer, use a duck puppet on the other hand to represent the mother.

SONG

Six Little Ducks

```
F                    C
Six little ducks that I once knew
C7                       F
Fat ones, skinny ones, pretty ones too.
```

Chorus

```
    But the one little duck with
        C
    The feather on his back,
    He ruled the others with his
        F
    "Quack, quack, quack!"
        C
    Quack, quack, quack!
        F
    Quack, quack, quack!
            C
    He ruled the others with his
        C           F
    "Quack, quack, quack!"


  F               C
Down to the water they would go
  C7                          F
Wibble, wabble, wibble, wabble to and fro.

    (repeat chorus)


  F               C
Up from the river they would come
  C7                          F
Wibble, wabble, wibble, wabble, oh, hum, hum.

    (repeat chorus)
```

CRAFT

Webbed Feet and Bill

Attach construction-paper cutouts of feet to construction-paper bands. Overlap the ends of the bands, and staple them together around children's ankles. (Enlist parents or caregivers to help with this.) Use thin poster board to make the bills. The children may color them and draw the nose holes. Punch holes in both sides of the bill. Tie strips of elastic or attach cut rubber bands to the holes. Show children how to wear the bills just above their mouths.

Supplies

orange construction paper
crayons or markers
poster board
elastic or rubber bands
staples
stapler

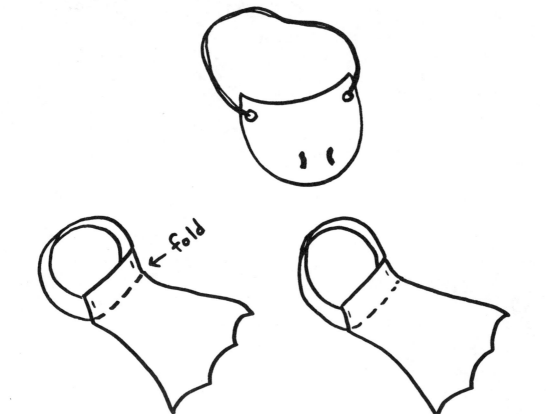

Penguin Parade

PUBLICITY

Celebrate the popular polar bird, the penguin, at the _____
Library on _____. We'll have penguin stories, penguin songs,
a penguin craft, and penguin fun! Call _____ to register.
Preschoolers, ages 3–6.

BOOK SUGGESTIONS

Geraghty, Paul. *Solo.*

Inkpen, Mick. *Penguin Small.*

Perlman, Janet. *The Emperor Penguin's New Clothes.*

Pfister, Marcus. *Penguin Pete, Ahoy!*

Vulliamy, Clara. *Ellen and Penguin.*

Wood, Audrey. *The Little Penguin's Tale.*

ACTION RHYMES

Five Perky Penguins

Five perky penguins
    (hold up five fingers)
Stood on the shore.
One went for a swim,
    (do swimming motions)
Then there were four.
    (hold up four fingers)

Four perky penguins
    (shade eyes with hand)
Looked out to sea.
    (look around)
One went swimming,
    (swimming motions)
And then there were three.
    (hold up three fingers)

Three perky penguins said,
"What can we do?"
One jumped into the water,
    (pretend to jump in water)
Then there were two.
    (hold up two fingers)

Two perky penguins
Sat in the sun.
One swam off,
    (swimming motions)
And then there was one.
    (hold up one finger)

One perky penguin said,
"This is no fun!"
He dived in the water,
    (diving motion)
And then there were none.

The Royal Penguin

The royal penguin waddles,
    (do a penguin walk)
On his funny webbed feet,
And he's the best dressed fellow,
You'd ever want to meet.

SONG

Laugh Little Penguin

(*Tune:* "Kookaburra")

The little penguin dives
In the sea so deep,
Catching all the fish
That he can eat.
Laugh, little penguin,
Laugh, little penguin,
Gay your life must be.

On his belly
He likes to slide,
All down the hill,
Just watch him glide.
Laugh, little penguin,
Laugh, little penguin,
Gay your life must be.

FLANNEL BOARD POEM

Five Little Penguins

Five little penguins,
As happy as could be,
Standing on a rock,
Looking out at the sea.

Crash! Went the waves,
Oh what a din!
Said the first little penguin,
"Shall we all jump in?"

Said the second little penguin,
"The water's like ice."
Said the third little penguin,
"That's not so nice."

Said the fourth little penguin,
"Let's bask in the sun."
Said the fifth little penguin,
"Hey, that's no fun!"

So the five little penguins
Took a leap and a dive,
And splashed into the water,
One, two, three, four, five.

Three seconds later,
Out they popped.
And stood once again
Atop that big rock.

Directions

Use the pattern to make five penguins out of felt. Cut a rock shape out of gray felt. Place the penguins on the flannel board in succession as you recite the poem. Jump them off the rock on: "Took a leap and a dive." Put them back on the rock at the end of the poem.

This poem may also be used with finger puppets. Reduce the pattern on a photocopier to a size appropriate for finger puppets. Make the penguins out of felt and attach them to the fingers of a glove with Velcro.

VIDEO

Show "The Tender Tale of Cinderella Penguin," which can be found on the video *The Tender Tale of Cinderella Penguin and Other Stories* from Smarty Pants Video (12 minutes).

CRAFT

Waddles, the Penguin

Cut penguin silhouettes out of heavy paper or poster board. Cut finger holes in the bottom. Let the children glue on wings, beaks, and eyes. Small cutouts of webbed feet may be taped to their fingers.

Going Ape

PUBLICITY

Come to the _____ Library for some monkeying
around on _____. Listen to ape stories, do monkey finger
plays, see a short video, and create a monkey mask. Call _____
to register. Preschoolers, ages 3–6.

BOOK SUGGESTIONS

Bodsworth, Nan. *Monkey Business*.
Bornstein, Ruth. *Little Gorilla*.
Brown, Anthony. *Gorilla*.
Christelow, Eileen. *Five Little
    Monkeys Sitting in a Tree*.

Morozumi, Atsuko. *One Gorilla*.
Slobodkina, Esphyr. *Caps for Sale*.
West, Colin. *"Not Me!" Said the
    Monkey*.

FINGER PLAY

Five Little Monkeys Jumping on the Bed

Five little monkeys jumping on the bed
  (jump fingers on the palm of other hand)
One fell off and bumped his head.
  (hold head in hands and move side to side)
Mommy called the doctor, and the doctor said,
  (pretend to dial phone)
No more monkeys jumping on the bed!
  (wag finger)

  (repeat with 4, 3, 2, and 1)

Put those monkeys straight to bed!

GAME

(Use this game with *Caps for Sale* by Slobodkina.)

Monkey See, Monkey Do

A little monkey likes to do,
Just the same as you and you.
  (suit actions to words)
When you climb a tree,
The monkey climbs a tree.
When you put on a hat,
The monkey puts on a hat.
When you stamp your feet,
The monkey stamps his feet.
When you throw your hat,
The monkey throws his hat.
And when you sit down,
The monkey sits down too.

—Lisa Renz

FINGER PUPPETS

Five Little Monkeys

Five little monkeys, sitting in a tree,
Teasing Mr. Crocodile: "You can't catch me!"
Along comes crocodile quiet as can be,
And, SNAP!

  (repeat with 4, 3, 2, and 1)

SNAP! Ha, ha, you missed me!

Directions

Use the following pattern to make five monkeys out of felt or poster board. Attach them to the fingers of a glove with Velcro. Use a crocodile sock puppet to snatch the monkeys off the glove, or you can use your hand to perform the same actions.

VIDEO

Show *Curious George* from Churchill Films (14 minutes).

CRAFT

Monkey Mask

Prior to the program, cut eye holes in paper plates and attach the plates to craft sticks. Let the children glue on a precut construction paper face and ears as shown. Let them use markers or crayons to color the plates and draw the nose and mouth.

Supplies

tan construction paper
markers or crayons
paper plates
craft sticks
glue

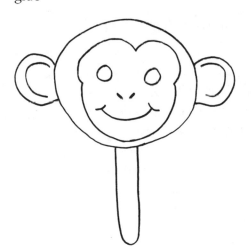

In the Days of the Dinosaurs

PUBLICITY

Travel back in time to when dinosaurs ruled the earth by joining us on
_____ at the _____ Library. Listen to
stories, sing dino songs, and do a dino craft. Call _____ to
register. Preschoolers, 3–6.

BOOK SUGGESTIONS

Blumenthal, Nancy. *Count-A-Saurus*.

Carrick, Carol. *Patrick's Dinosaurs*.

Cauley, Lorinda Bryan. *The Trouble with Tyrannosaurus Rex*.

Most, Bernard. *If the Dinosaurs Came Back*.

Mullins, Patricia. *Dinosaur Encore*.

Sirois, Allen. *Dinosaur Dress Up*.

Stickland, Paul. *Dinosaur Roar!*

FINGER PLAY

Five Tremendous Dinosaurs

Five tremendous dinosaurs
*(hold up five fingers and extend
arms wide)*
Letting out a roar.
*(cup hands over mouth and
roar)*
One ran away,
(hold up one finger)
And then there were four.
(hold up four fingers)

Four tremendous dinosaurs
(extend arms)
Crashing down a tree.
(stamp feet)
One went away,
(hold up one finger)
And then there were three.
(hold up three fingers)

Three tremendous dinosaurs
(extend arms)
Eating tiger stew.
(pretend to chew)
One went away,
(hold up one finger)
Then there were two.
(hold up two fingers)

Two tremendous dinosaurs
(extend arms)
Having lots of fun,
'Til a volcano blew up,
(push both arms above head)
And then there was one.
(hold up one finger)

One tremendous dinosaur,
He must have weighed a ton.
(extend arms)
He went to join his friends,
And then there were none!

ACTION RHYME

The Enormous Brontosaurus

The enormous brontosaurus is as tall
as can be.
(extend one arm high over head)
Her lunch is a bunch of leaves off a
tree.
*(make nibbling motion with
fingers)*
She has a very long neck, and her
tail is long too.
*(put arms together and swish
them to indicate long tail)*
And she is much, much too large to
fit in the zoo.
(extend arms wide)

SONG

Bringing Home a Baby Dinosaur

(*Tune:* "I'm Bringing Home a Baby
Bumblebee")

Oh, I'm bringing home a baby
dinosaur.
Won't my mommy fall right through
the floor?
Cause I'm bringing home a baby
dinosaur.
ROAR!!!
Boy, is he noisy!

DRAWING STORY

Cretaceous Hill

One fine morning Julie and Josh went on a hike in the woods. There was a hill they wanted to climb because they had heard fossils could be found there. It was called Cretaceous Hill. This is the hill.

Julie and Josh climbed the hill and scouted around for fossils, but they didn't find any. When they got to the top, they admired the view. At the base of the hill they saw tall grass growing and an old tree that had lost all its leaves.

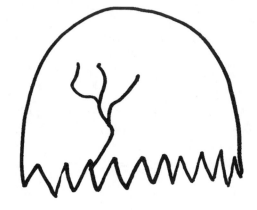

In the distance, far below, Julie thought she could see something round and white shining in the sunlight.

"Let's run down the hill and see what that thing is, Josh!" said Julie.

"OK," said Josh. "Let's race down. You run down that side of the hill and I'll run down this side."

"All right! Last one down is a rotten egg!" yelled Julie.

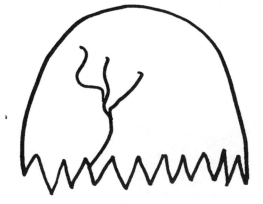

Well, Julie ran down this way and Josh ran down that way. Josh was running so fast he went past the shiny white thing and into a swampy area. Then he came back around and tripped over two stones, and he finally met Julie.

"I guess you're the rotten egg," laughed Julie.

"Oh, look!" cried Josh. "I think it's a fossilized dinosaur egg!"

"Wait a minute," said Julie. "I think it's cracking open!"

Julie

Josh

Stones

Swampy area

Suddenly the egg cracked wide open and out came a baby dinosaur!

(Turn the drawing around when you say "baby dinosaur" and add details to the mouth and eye.)

VIDEO

Show *Danny and the Dinosaur* from Children's Circle (8 minutes).

CRAFT

The Baby Dinosaur

Precut the dinosaurs and egg pieces out of heavy paper. Make a small hole so that children can attach the egg pieces with brads. Let the children color the dinosaurs and glue them to the eggs. Googly eyes may be added to the face.

Supplies

construction paper
heavy white paper
washable markers
googly eyes
brads
glue

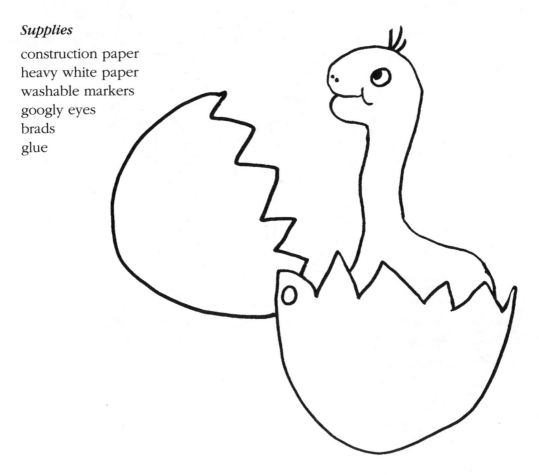

Mooo!

PUBLICITY

"What did the cow say when the barn got crowded?" "Mooove over!"
Join us down on the farm at the _____ Library
on _____ for some great farm stories and songs. Call
_____ to register. Preschoolers, ages 3–6.

BOOK SUGGESTIONS

Allen, Pamela. *Belinda*.

Hellen, Nancy. *Old MacDonald Had a Farm*.

Hill, Eric. *Spot on the Farm*.

King, Bob. *Sitting on the Farm*.

MacLachlan, Patricia. *All the Places to Love*.

Tafuri, Nancy. *This Is the Farmer*.

Waddell, Martin. *Farmer Duck*.

Wood, Jakki. *Moo, Moo, Brown Cow*.

Zimmerman, Andrea. *The Cow Buzzed*.

ACTION RHYME

Five Little Farmers

Five little farmers
   (hold up five fingers)
Woke up with the sun,
   (arms circle over head)
For it was early morning
And chores must be done.

The first little farmer
Went to milk the cow.
   (do milking motion)
The second little farmer
Thought he'd better plow.
   (pretend to plow)

The third little farmer
Fed the hungry hens.
   (pretend to toss out feed)
The fourth little farmer
Mended broken pens.
   (pretend to hammer)

The fifth little farmer
Took his vegetables to town.
   *(hold imaginary steering wheel
   and pretend to drive)*
Baskets filled with cabbages
And sweet potatoes, brown.

When the work was finished
And the western sky was red,
Five little farmers
Tumbled into bed.
   (rest head on hands)

FINGER PLAYS

The Boy in the Barn

A little boy went into a barn,
   (hold up index finger)
And lay down on some hay,
   (lay finger down on other hand)
An owl came in and flew about,
   *(cross wrists and thumbs and
   flap fingers)*
And the little boy ran away.
   (hide index finger behind back)

The Little Cow

This little cow eats grass,
   *(hold up hand with all fingers
   straight and wiggle little finger)*
This little cow eats hay,
   (wiggle ring finger)
This little cow looks over the hedge,
   (wiggle middle finger)
This little cow runs away,
   (wiggle index finger)
And this BIG cow does nothing at all
   (wiggle thumb)
But lie in the fields all day!
   *(touch five fingers in succession
   starting with thumb)*

FLANNEL BOARD SONG

Old MacDonald

Enlarge the patterns on a photo-copier to the size you prefer. Sing "Old MacDonald" as you place the animals on the flannel board. For tips on making story figures, see the section on flannel board storytelling in the introduction.

SONG

Old MacDonald

Chorus

Old MacDonald had a farm,
E-I-E-I-O!

And on this farm he had some
    chicks,
E-I-E-I-O!
With a chick, chick here,
And a chick, chick there,
Here a chick, there a chick,
Everywhere a chick, chick.

(repeat chorus)

(*continue with* ducks . . . quack . . .
sheep . . . baa
pigs . . . oink
cow . . . moo
dog . . . bow wow)

VIDEO

Show *The Big Red Barn* from Paramount Communications (10 minutes).

CRAFT

Clothespin Cow

Provide each child with a cow silhouette cut from thin poster board or heavy paper. Let children color their cows and add details such as eyes and a mouth. They can glue or tape on a thick string tail and fray the end of it to create a tassel. Have children clip on the clothespins so the cow can stand.

Supplies

thin poster board or heavy paper
thick string
clothespins
washable markers

Teddy Bear Tea

PUBLICITY

Preschoolers, bring your teddy bears to the _____
Library on _____ and join us for stories, songs, and a beary,
beary good time. Dress in fancy clothes if you like, and bring six cookies to
share. We're having a tea party! Call _____ to register.

BOOK SUGGESTIONS

Asch, Frank. *Mooncake.*

Butler, Dorothy. *My Brown Bear
    Barney.*

Degen, Bruce. *Jamberry.*

Douglass, Barbara. *Good as New.*

Galdone, Paul. *The Three Bears.*

Newman, Nanette. *There's a Bear in
    the Bath.*

Wood, Jakki. *One Bear with Bees in
    His Hair.*

ACTION RHYME

Bear Hunt

I'm going on a bear hunt.
I'm going on a bear hunt.
   (slap thighs alternately)
I see a swamp.
   (shade eyes with hands)
Can't go under it,
Can't go over it,
   (slap thighs)
Have to go through it.
Slush, slush, slush, slush.
   (rub hands together)

I'm going on a bear hunt.
I'm going on a bear hunt.
   (slap thighs)
I see a bridge.
   (shade eyes with hands)
Can't go under it,
Can't go through it,
   (slap thighs)
Have to go over it.
Thump, thump, thump, thump.
   (stamp feet)

I'm going on a bear hunt.
I'm going on a bear hunt.
   (slap thighs)
I see a stream.
   (shade eyes with hands)
Can't go under it,
Can't go over it,
   (slap thighs)
Have to go through it.
Splash, splash, splash, splash.
   (do swim strokes)

I'm going on a bear hunt.
I'm going on a bear hunt.
   (slap thighs)
I see a tree.
   (shade eyes with hand)
Let's go see.
   (slap thighs)
Up, up, up, up.
   (climbing motion)

I see a cave.
   (shade eyes with hand)
Down, down, down, down.
   (climbing down motion)
Let's go see.
   (slap thighs)

I feel something.
   (feel with hands)
I feel something furry.
It feels like a bear.
It looks like a bear.
It IS a bear!
   (quickly slap thighs)

Up.
   (climb up)
Down.
   (climb down)
Splash, splash, splash.
   (swim strokes)
Thump, thump, thump.
   (stamp feet)
Slush, slush, slush.
   (rub hands together)
Woo!!!
   (collapse)
I'm not going on a bear hunt again!

FINGER PLAY

Here Is a Cave

Here is a cave.
   (bend fingers on one hand)
Inside is a bear.
   *(put thumb of same hand inside
   fingers)*
Now he comes out
   (pop out thumb)
To get some fresh air.

He stays out all summer
In sunshine and heat.
He hunts in the forest
For berries to eat.
   (move thumb in a circle)

When the snow starts to fall,
He hurries inside
His warm little cave,
And there he will hide.
   (put thumb inside fingers)

Snow covers the cave,
   (place one hand over other)
Like a fluffy white rug.
Inside the bear sleeps,
All cozy and snug.

FINGER PUPPETS

This Little Bear

This little bear has a soft fur suit.
This little bear acts very cute.
This little bear is bold and cross.
This little bear thinks he's the boss.
This little bear likes bacon and
   honey,
But he can't buy them. He has no
   money.

Directions

Use the pattern to make five bears
out of felt or poster board. Attach
Velcro to the back of each bear and
to the fingers of a glove.

ACTION RHYME

Teddy Bear, Teddy Bear

Teddy Bear, Teddy Bear, turn around.
(suit actions to words)
Teddy Bear, Teddy Bear, touch the
ground.
Teddy Bear, Teddy Bear, dance on
your toes.
Teddy Bear, Teddy Bear, touch your
nose.
Teddy Bear, Teddy Bear, climb the
stairs.
Teddy Bear, Teddy Bear, say your
prayers.
Teddy Bear, Teddy Bear, turn out the
light.
Teddy Bear, Teddy Bear, say good
night.

VIDEO

Show *Goldilocks and the Three Bears*
from Weston Woods (8 minutes).

SONG

The Bear Went over the Mountain

(*Tune:* "For He's a Jolly Good
Fellow")

The bear went over the mountain,
The bear went over the mountain,
The bear went over the mountain,
To see what he could see.

And all that he could see,
And all that he could see
Was another mountain,
Was another mountain,
Was another mountain,
And what do you think he did?

He climbed the other mountain,
He climbed the other mountain,
He climbed the other mountain,
To see what he could see.

(*Repeat second and third verses
alternately. End with* "And what
do you think he did?")

(*spoken*)

He fell fast asleep.
Why, why, why?
Because he had climbed so many
mountains!

ACTIVITY

Teddy Bear Tea

Set up tables with fancy tablecloths,
centerpieces, real cups and saucers,
and plates for the cookies. If possible, have someone dressed in a bear
costume go around with a teapot
and serve tea. Pasteurized apple
juice may be substituted for tea.

I Like Spiders
and Snakes

PUBLICITY

If you think snakes are sensational and spiders are special, come to the
_____ Library on _____. We will
celebrate these creepy crawlies with story, song, and a craft activity.
Call _____ to register. Preschoolers, ages 3–6.

BOOK SUGGESTIONS

Kimmel, Eric A. *Anansi and the Moss-Covered Rock.*

Kirk, David. *Miss Spider's Tea Party.*

Kudrna, Charlene Imbior. *To Bathe a Boa.*

McNulty, Faith. *Snake in the House.*

Trapani, Iza. *The Itsy Bitsy Spider.*

Walsh, Ellen. *Mouse Count.*

ACTION RHYME

Spider Web

I'm a big spider.
(stand and hold arms out with hands open)
I spin, I spin,
(turn in place)
I spin big webs,
To catch little flies in.
(bring arms to chest)

FINGER PLAY

The Little Snake

Slithering, sliding, slinking,
(place palms together and make a slithering motion)
Comes the little snake.
In and out goes her tongue,
(make tongue go in and out)
What a great pet she'd make!

SONG

I'm Being Swallowed by a Boa Constrictor

Sing "I'm Being Swallowed by a Boa Constrictor." Peter, Paul, and Mary sing this on their album *Peter, Paul, and Mommy*. The words are by Shel Silverstein and can be found in *Where the Sidewalk Ends* on page 45.

FLANNEL BOARD STORY

Spider and the Magic Stone

The instructions and patterns for this story can be found on page 65.

CREATIVE DRAMATICS

Little Miss Muffet

Act out the Mother Goose rhyme "Little Miss Muffet" using a spider on a stick (see craft). Give several children a chance to act out the rhyme in front of the group.

Little Miss Muffet
Sat on a tuffet,
Eating her curds and whey;
Along came a big spider,
And sat down beside her,
And frightened Miss Muffet away.

—Mother Goose

VIDEO

Show *The Day Jimmy's Boa Ate the Wash* from Weston Woods (8 minutes).

CRAFT

Spider on a Stick

Before the program, paint small Styrofoam balls black, and staple and glue elastic or string to the balls. Let the children push black pipe cleaners into the balls to create legs and glue on googly eyes. Help children tie the other end of the string to craft sticks.

Supplies

black pipe cleaners
elastic or string
Styrofoam balls
craft sticks
googly eyes
black paint
glue

Under the Sea

PUBLICITY

Join us on an undersea adventure at the _____
Library on _____. Enjoy stories, poems, and songs about
sharks, octopuses, whales, and other wondrous creatures of the deep.
Create a glittering fish to take home. Call _____ to register.
Preschoolers, ages 3–6.

BOOK SUGGESTIONS

MacCarthy, Patricia. *Ocean Parade: A Counting Book.*

Martin, Antoinette. *Famous Seaweed Soup.*

Mellor, Corrine. *Clark the Toothless Shark.*

Morris, Winifred. *What if the Shark Wears Tennis Shoes?*

Raffi. *Baby Beluga.*

Sheldon, Dyan. *Whale Song.*

Wu, Norbert. *Fish Faces.*

ACTION RHYME

Slippery Fish

Slippery fish, slippery fish,
  *(make wavy swimming motions
    with hands)*
Sliding through the water.
Slippery fish, slippery fish,
  (wavy motions)
Glup, glup, glup.
  *(make a snapping motion with
    palms together)*
Oh, no! He's been eaten by a . . .

Tuna fish, tuna fish,
  *(make snapping motion with
    palms)*
Swimming through the water.
Tuna fish, tuna fish,
Glup, glup, glup.
  (snapping motions with palms)
Oh, no! He's been eaten by an . . .

Octopus, octopus,
  (wiggle arms around)
Wriggling through the water.
Octopus, octopus,
Glup, glup, glup.
Oh, no! He's been eaten by a . . .

Great white shark,
  *(with elbows together, bring
    forearms together like a jaw
    snapping)*
Lurking through the water.
Great white shark,
Glup, glup, glup.
Oh, no! He's been eaten by a . . .

Humungous whale,
  *(open and close outstretched
    arms to indicate a whale's jaws)*
Spouting through the water.

FINGER PLAY

Goldfish

My darling little goldfish
Hasn't any toes.
  (point to toes)
He swims around without a sound
  *(make wavy motions with right
    hand)*
And bumps his hungry nose.
  (tap nose with right hand)
He can't get out and play with me
  (right hand swimming motion)
Nor I get in to him.
  (left hand stands upright)
Although I say, "Come out and
  play,"
  (left hand beckons to right hand)
He says, "Come in and swim."
  (right hand beckons to left hand)

SONG

Row, Row, Row Your Boat

Row, row, row your boat,
  *(do rowing motions while you
    sing this song)*
Gently down the stream.
Merrily, merrily, merrily, merrily,
Life is but a dream.

OVERHEAD PROJECTOR POEM

The Fish with the Deep Sea Smile

This poem can be found in *Nibble, Nibble: Poems for Children* by Margaret Wise Brown.

Enlarge the patterns on a photocopier. Trace them onto transparen-cies with a permanent marker or, if possible, use your photocopier to copy the patterns onto transparencies. Add colors with red, green, blue, or yellow overhead-projector pens. Trace or photocopy the fishermen onto the top of a transparency sheet and draw a water line in blue as shown in the illustration. You may also want to draw a little seaweed or small sea creatures on the bottom. Tape the transparency to the overhead so it won't shift during the presentation.

Trace or photocopy the fish onto separate transparencies (you may need two sheets for all the fish), add color, and cut them out. Tape clear drinking straws perpendicularly to the backs of the fish. This will enable you to move them around in the "water."

As you recite the poem, add and remove each fish at the appropriate time. Practice the presentation at least once before performing in front of an audience.

Supplies

overhead projector
transparencies
permanent marker
overhead projector pens
    (various colors)
clear drinking straws
tape
scissors

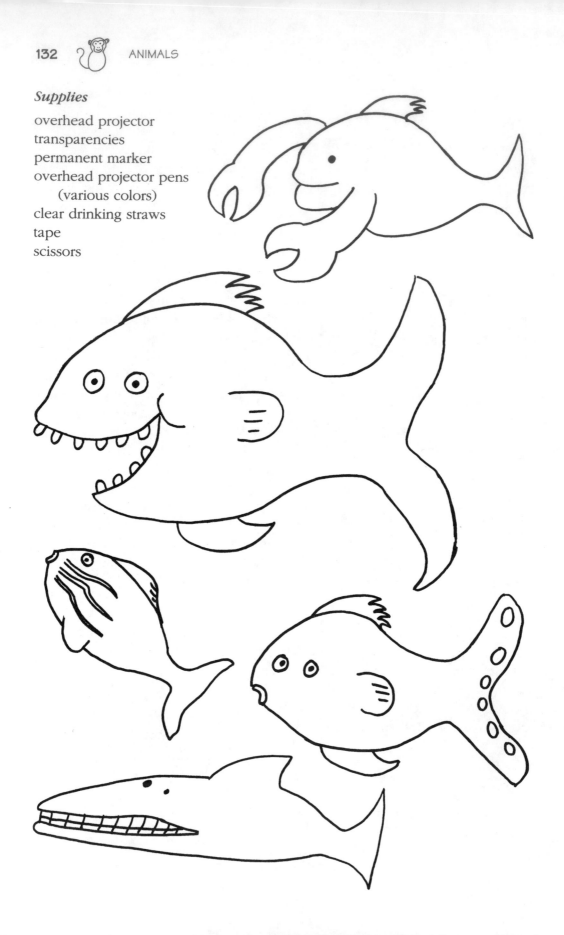

ACTIVITY

Swimming to Music

Practice swim strokes with your group by "swimming" around the room. Do the backstroke, the side-stroke, the butterfly stroke, the Australian crawl, or anything else you can think of. Some suggestions for music to play during this activity are "Under the Sea" (Disney) and "Octopus's Garden" (The Beatles).

VIDEO

Show *Swimmy* from Lucerne Films (6 minutes).

CRAFT

Glittering Fish

Provide children with fish silhou-ettes. Let them add details using var-ious materials you have on hand, such as sequins, shiny wrapping paper, googly eyes, and glitter.

Supplies

shiny wrapping paper
fish silhouettes
googly eyes
sequins
glitter
glue

PART FOUR

HODGEPODGE

The Magic Pasta Pot

PUBLICITY

Preschoolers and parents or caregivers, bring your appetite to the
_____ Library on _____. Listen to
stories about pasta, sing spaghetti songs, see a short video, and enjoy a
delicious pasta feast. Call _____ to register. Preschoolers,
ages 3–6.

BOOK SUGGESTIONS

Barrett, Judi. *Cloudy with a Chance of Meatballs.*

Cocca-Leffler, Maryann. *Wednesday Is Spaghetti Day.*

Coplans, Peta. *Spaghetti for Suzy.*

De Paola, Tomie. *Strega Nona.*

Hines, Anna Grossnickle. *Daddy Makes the Best Spaghetti.*

ACTION RHYME

Pasta in a Pot

I like pasta nice and hot.
(pretend to blow on a plate of pasta)
I like pasta with cheese.
(pretend to sprinkle cheese)
I like pasta in a pot,
(make a circle with arms)
With meatballs if you please.
(make circles by joining index fingers to thumbs)
Give me lots of sauce,
(pretend to ladle sauce)
And some garlic bread too,
(hold out hand)
And a big glass of milk.
(pretend to drink)
Thanks! That will do!
(rub tummy)

SONG

On Top of Spaghetti

Sing "On Top of Spaghetti" and don't forget to do a real sneeze. The song can be found in *Eye Winker, Tom Tinker, Chin Chopper* by Tom Glazer. The musical arrangement and guitar chords are included.

ACTIVITY

Pasta Feast

Cover tables with red-checked tablecloths, play Italian music, and serve up bowls of lightly buttered pasta. (Avoid tomato sauce—less mess.) You may want to serve the pasta out of a large black kettle similar to Strega Nonna's.

MUSICAL ACTION RHYME

Spaghetti, Meatballs, and Cheese

(*Tune:* "Peanut Butter and Jelly")

Chorus

Spaghetti, spaghetti and meatballs, and cheese!
Spaghetti, spaghetti and meatballs, and cheese!

First you make the sauce and you stir it,
(suit actions to words)
You stir it, you stir it, stir it, stir it, singing:

(repeat chorus after each verse)

Then you make the meatballs and you roll them . . .
Then you take the spaghetti and you boil it . . .
Then you take some cheese and you sprinkle it . . .
Then you eat the spaghetti and you slurp it . . .
(use appropriate sound effects)
Then you get some milk and you glug it . . .

VIDEO

Show *Strega Nona* from Children's Circle (10 minutes).

Toys, Toys, Toys

PUBLICITY

Delight in stories about toys at the _____
Library on _____. See a short video and make a spinning
top to take home. Call _____ to register. Preschoolers,
ages 3–6.

BOOK SUGGESTIONS

Dale, Penny. *Ten out of Bed.*

Douglass, Barbara. *Good as New.*

Galbraith, Kathryn O. *Laura
    Charlotte.*

Goodspeed, Peter. *A Rhinoceros
    Wakes Me Up in the Morning.*

Hissey, Jane. *Jolly Snow.*

Inkpen, Mick. *Kipper's Toybox.*

Paxton, Tom. *The Marvelous Toy.*

Vulliamy, Clara. *Ellen and Penguin.*

Waddell, Martin. *The Toymaker.*

ACTION RHYMES

Jack-in-the-Box

Jack-in-the-box all shut up tight,
> *(squat down with hands on head)*

Not a breath of air, not a ray of light.
How dark it must be, he cannot see,
Open the box and up jumps he!
> *(lift hands and jump up)*

Rag Doll

Let's play rag doll,
Let's not make a sound.
Fling your arms and body
> *(suit actions to words)*

Loosely around.
Fling your arms and your feet,
And let your head go free,
Be the raggediest rag doll,
You ever did see.

SONG

Marvelous Toy

Play Tom Paxton's song "Marvelous Toy," which can be found on his album *Marvelous Toy and Other Gallimaufry*. This song can also be found on Peter, Paul, and Mary's album *Peter, Paul, and Mommy*.

FLANNEL BOARD POEM

The Toy Shop

For the poem, patterns, and directions see pages 44–5.

VIDEO

Show *The Tin Toy* from Direct Cinema (5 minutes).

CRAFT

Make a Top

Let children decorate the bottom of two small paper plates with colored markers. When they are finished, have them bring their plates to you so you can poke holes in the middle of the plates, tape the rims together, and push a sharpened pencil through the holes. (The pointed end should stick out an inch or so.) Show children how to roll the pencil between their hands and then let go to make the top spin.

Supplies

paper plates
sharpened pencils
washable markers
tape

Outerspace Adventure

PUBLICITY

Venture into space where no one has gone before at the _____

Library on _____. Listen to stories about space and

space travel, sing songs, see a short video, and create a flying saucer.

Call _____ to register. Preschoolers, ages 3–6.

BOOK SUGGESTIONS

Asch, Frank. *Mooncake.*

Barton, Byron. *I Want to Be an Astronaut.*

Carle, Eric. *Papa, Please Get the Moon for Me.*

McNaughton, Colin. *Here Come the Aliens!*

Marshall, Edward. *Space Case.*

Sadler, Marilyn. *Alistair in Outer Space.*

Young, Ruth. *A Trip to Mars.*

ACTION RHYME

Blastoff

Jump into your spacesuit.
Don't forget your hat.
  *(pretend to put on suit and
    helmet)*
Buckle up for take off,
Belts from head to toe.
  (pretend to buckle up)
Count down for ten and blast off,
Up to the moon we go!
10, 9, 8, 7, 6, 5, 4, 3, 2, 1 . . .
Blastoff!
  *(count on fingers, put palms
    together, and extend arms above
    head)*

FINGER PLAY

Rocket Ship

Inside the rocket ship
Not much room.
Ready for countdown,
10, 9, 8, 7, 6, 5, 4, 3, 2, 1 ZOOM!
  *(count on fingers, place palms
    together, and extend arms
    overhead)*

FINGER PUPPETS

Five Flying Saucer Men

Five flying saucer men came out the
  spaceship door,
One did a somersault, then there
  were four.
Four flying saucer men, as odd as
  they could be,
One fell over backward, and then
  there were three.
Three flying saucer men with skin of
  green and blue,
One rode on a space monster, and
  then there were two.
Two flying saucer men were having
  such fun,
One beamed up, and then there was
  one.
One flying saucer man on Earth all
  alone,
He missed all his buddies, so he
  went on home.

Directions

Use the pattern provided to make five finger puppets out of felt. Vary the expressions on each puppet's face. Use googly eyes if desired. Attach Velcro to the backs of the puppets and to the fingers of a glove.

SONG

Twinkle, Twinkle, Little Star

   D   D7   G   D
Twinkle, twinkle, little star,

 A7   D   A7   D
How I wonder what you are.

 D   A7   D   A7
Up above the world so high,

 D   A7   D   A7
Like a diamond in the sky.

   D   D7   G   B7
Twinkle, twinkle, little star,

 Em   D   A7   D
How I wonder what you are.

VIDEO

Show *The Mole and the Green Star* from McGraw-Hill (8 minutes).

CRAFT

Flying Saucer

Before the program, tape together the rims of two paper plates, and attach a small paper cup or bowl to the top. Let the children decorate their ships with markers. Suggest that when they go home they can fly them outside. Explain that the saucers will fly something like a Frisbee when tossed.

Supplies

paper cups or bowls
paper plates
washable markers
tape

Teeny Tiny Tales and Giant Adventures

PUBLICITY

Fee, Fi, Fo, Fum! To the _____ Library you must come. We will have stories about the very, very small and the very, very tall, with a short video and a fun craft activity to boot. Call _____ to register. Preschoolers, ages 3–6.

BOOK SUGGESTIONS

Cauley, Lorinda Bryan. *Jack and the Beanstalk.*

Galdone, Paul. *The Teeny-Tiny Woman: A Ghost Story.*

Geraghty, Paul. *Look Out Patrick!*

Kraus, Robert. *The Little Giant.*

Lobel, Arnold. *Giant John.*

Pearson, Susan. *Jack and the Beanstalk.*

Seeger, Pete. *Abiyoyo.*

Severn, Jeffrey. *George and His Giant Shadow.*

ACTION RHYMES

Poof! I'm a Giant

Poof! I'm a giant. Huge in size.
   (stand up tall)
Poof! I'm an owl with big yellow
   eyes.
   (fingers circle eyes)
Poof! I'm a mouse with an ee ee ee!
   (squat down)
Poof! This is best,
Now I'm back to me.
   (stand up)

Tall as a Tree

Tall as a tree,
   (reach for the ceiling)
Wide as a house,
   (reach toward walls)
Thin as a pin,
   (place arms next to body)
Small as a mouse.
   *(squat down and make self
   small)*

FINGER PLAY

Mouse in a Hole

A mouse lived in a little hole,
   (tuck thumb in fist)
Lived softly in a little hole
When it was quiet as can be . . .
Out popped he!
   *(pop thumb out of
   fist)*

FLANNEL BOARD STORY

The Teeny Tiny Woman

Many versions of the story "The Teeny Tiny Woman" can be found in folk tale collections such as *English Fairy Tales* by Joseph Jacobs and in picture-book format such as Paul Galdone's *The Teeny-Tiny Woman: A Ghost Story* or Barbara Seuling's *The Teeny Tiny Woman: An Old English Ghost Tale.* Use the patterns to create story figures out of felt. For tips on how to make story figures, see the section on flannel board storytelling in the introduction.

SONG

Abiyoyo

Read *Abiyoyo* by Pete Seeger and sing the song "Abiyoyo." The music is on the last page of the book. The song can also be found on Seeger's *Abiyoyo and Other Story Songs for Children* album.

VIDEO

Show *Dr. De Soto* from Weston Woods (10 minutes).

CRAFT

Jack and the Beanstalk

Prior to the program, acquire a supply of paper towel tubes and paint them green. After reading "Jack and the Beanstalk" to children, let them glue precut leaves onto the "beanstalk." Give them rough-cut body silhouettes of the Giant and Jack, and let them draw and color the details such as faces and clothing and glue them onto the beanstalk.

Supplies

construction paper
paper towel tubes
washable markers
glue
green paint
crayons

Ride 'em Cowboy

PUBLICITY

Preschoolers (and parents or caregivers), wear your ten-gallon hats and come to the _____ Library for an old West adventure out on the range. We'll have a rip-roaring roundup of wild West tales, songs, and activities for your enjoyment. This will all happen on _____. Please call _____ to register.

BOOK SUGGESTIONS

Birney, Betty G. *Tyrannosaurus Tex.*
Brett, Jan. *Armadillo Rodeo.*
Kellogg, Steven. *Pecos Bill.*
Mayer, Mercer. *Cowboy Critter.*
Medearis, Angela Shelf. *The Zebra-Riding Cowboy: A Folk Song from the Old West.*

Rounds, Glen. *Cowboys.*
Yorinks, Arthur. *Whitefish Will Rides Again.*

ACTION RHYME

Cowboy Billy

Cowboy Billy
Went to Philly
Hands up! Stick 'em up!
   (hold hands up)
Cowboy Billy,
Cowboy Billy
Broke his toe
   (hold toe and hop around on
     one foot)
Riding on a wild bronco.
Cowboy Billy,
Cowboy Billy
His spine went crack
   (place hands on lower back)
Riding on a buffalo's back.
Poor Cowboy Billy.

SONGS

Home on the Range

     C
Oh, give me a home
          F
Where the buffalo roam
         C   G
And the deer and the antelope play.
      C
Where seldom is heard
     F
A discouraging word
          C   G   C
And the skies are not cloudy all day

   G   C
Home, home on the range
                            G
Where the deer and the antelope play
      C
Where seldom is heard
     F
A discouraging word
          C   G   C
And the skies are not cloudy all day.

Buffalo Gals

D
As I was a-walking down the street,
  A7   D
Down the street, down the street,
A7 D
A pretty girl I chanced to meet,
  G   A7   D
Under the silvery moon.

Chorus

  D
Buffalo gals, won't you come out tonight,
   A   D
Come out tonight, come out tonight.
Buffalo gals, won't you come out tonight
       G   A7   D
and dance by the light of the moon.

I asked her if she'd stop and talk,
Stop and talk, Stop and talk,
Her feet covered up the whole sidewalk,
She was fair to view.

(repeat chorus)

CRAFT

Shoe Box Guitar

Ask program participants to bring empty shoe boxes to the program. Cut circular holes in the shoe box lids for the children. Help them wrap large rubber bands around the boxes and attach paper towel tubes (guitar necks) with tape.

Supplies

paper towel tubes
rubber bands
shoe boxes
tape

ACTIVITY

Campfire Songs

Prepare an imitation campfire before you do the program. Attach some red and yellow construction paper flames to a few logs. At the end of the program sing cowboy songs such as "The Old Chisholm Trail" and "Happy Trails" found on *The Cowboy Album,* and play shoe box guitars (see craft) around the campfire.

Pirates and Parrots

PUBLICITY

"Shiver me timbers and blow me down," come to the _____
Library on _____. We'll have stories about pirates and parrots,
sing seafaring songs, create a treasure chest, and hunt for hidden
treasures. Call _____ to register. Preschoolers, ages 3–6.

BOOK SUGGESTIONS

Burningham, John. *Come Away from the Water, Shirley.*

Cole, Babette. *The Trouble with Uncle.*

Fox, Mem. *Tough Boris.*

Hutchins, Pat. *One-Eyed Jake.*

McDermott, Gerald. *Papagayo the Mischief Maker.*

Ross, Tony. *The Treasure of Cozy Cove.*

Tucker, Kathy. *Do Pirates Take Baths?*

Zacharias, Thomas and Wanda. *But Where Is the Green Parrot?*

ACTION RHYME

One-Eyed Pirate

The one-eyed pirate,
    (cover one eye)
He's fierce and he's tough,
    (clench fists)
He digs for buried treasure.
    (digging motion)
He never finds enough.

He lives on a ship,
Way out on the sea.
    (make wavy motion with hand)
His parrot is his only friend,
    (perch hand on shoulder)
Except for me.
    (point to self)

FINGER PLAY

Parrots on a Pirate

Two green parrots on a pirate
    perched,
    (perch hands on shoulders)
One flew away and then there was
    one.
    *(fly one hand away behind
    back)*
The other flew after,
    *(fly other hand away behind
    back)*
And then there was none.

Of those two parrots, one back
    again flew.
    (put one hand back on shoulder)
The other flew after, and then there
    were two.
    *(put other hand back on
    shoulder)*
Said the pirate to the parrots,
"Do you want a cracker, Polly?"
Said the parrots to the pirate,
    *(make talking motion with
    hands)*
"Yes we do, by golly!"

SONG

Blow the Man Down

    C
Come all you young fellows that follow the sea,
        Am Dm   G7
With a way, hey, blow the man down,
                  Dm
Now please pay attention and listen to me,
 G7   C
Give me some time to blow the man down.

CRAFT

Treasure Chest

Obtain a supply of shoeboxes from local shoe stores and paint them black. Let the children decorate them with precut skulls and crossbones, sequins, and other craft materials that can be glued on.

Supplies

precut skulls and crossbones
shoe boxes
black paint
sequins
glue

ACTIVITY

Treasure Hunt

Hide craft beads, foil-covered cardboard coins (pieces of eight), and other small "treasures" around the room. At the end of the program, let the children hunt for the treasures and put them in their treasure chests to take home.

On the Road

PUBLICITY

Come join us for a road rally at the _____ Library
on _____. Enjoy stories and songs about automobiles and
make your own "box" car. Call _____ to register. Preschoolers,
ages 3–6.

BOOK SUGGESTIONS

Burningham, John. *Mr. Gumpy's Motor Car.*

Crews, Donald. *School Bus.*

Fowler, Richard. *Cat's Car.*

Hellen, Mary. *The Bus Stop.*

Siebert, Diane. *Truck Song.*

Stott, Dorothy. *Little Duck's Bicycle Ride.*

Zelinsky, Paul O. *Wheels on the Bus.*

FINGER PLAY

I'm a Little Sports Car

I'm a little sports car,
Shiny and yellow.
When I go out driving,
    (pretend to drive)
I'm a very happy fellow.

When the rain comes down,
    (flutter fingers downward)
I turn my wipers on.
    (move arms back and forth)
It's fun to splash through puddles,
All around the town.

When I see a red light,
I stop on a dime.
    (stop moving)
When I see a green light,
I know it's driving time.
    (move forward)
Beep! Beep!

SONG

Wheels on the Bus

The wheels on the bus go 'round
    and 'round,
    (suit actions to words)
'Round and 'round, 'round and
    'round.
The wheels on the bus go 'round
    and 'round,
All around the town.

The wipers on the bus go swish,
    swish, swish . . .
The horn on the bus goes beep,
    beep, beep . . .
The babies on the bus go waa, waa,
    waa . . .
The mommies on the bus go shh,
    shh, shh . . .

VIDEO

Show *Susie the Little Blue Coupe*
from Walt Disney (8 minutes).

CRAFT

Box Car

Prior to the program, make a road
around the room by putting down
masking-tape lanes. Ask all participants to bring a child-sized cardboard box with the top and bottom
cut out to the program. With the
assistance of parent helpers each
child will construct a car using the
box, construction paper for wheels,
license plates, taillights, and controls;
aluminum foil for headlights; and
paper plates and brads for steering
wheels.

After the car is completed let the
children motor around the room by
holding their cars up around their
midsections and walking around the
room on the "road." Play car songs,
such as "Car, Car Song" on Fred
Penner's *Ebeneezer Sneezer* album or
"Riding in My Car" on Pete Seeger's
Children's Concert at Town Hall
album, on a tape player.

Supplies

construction paper
cardboard box with the top and
    bottom cut out
paper plates and brads
aluminum foil
glue
tape

Yummy in
My Tummy

PUBLICITY

Come to the _____ Library on _____
for stories, songs, and poems that are sure to whet your appetite. Call
_____ to register. Preschoolers, ages 3–6.

BOOK SUGGESTIONS

Bender, Robert. *A Most Unusual Lunch*.

Demarest, Chris. *No Peas for Nellie*.

Hutchins, Pat. *The Doorbell Rang*.

Kasza, Keiko. *The Wolf's Chicken Stew*.

Shaw, Nancy. *Sheep out to Eat*.

Shelby, Anne. *Potluck*.

Spurr, Elizabeth. *The Gumdrop Tree*.

Tanis, Joel E. *The Dragon Pack Snack Attack*.

FINGER PLAY

Who Stole the Cookies?

Who stole the cookies from the
  cookie jar?
Number one stole the cookies from
  the cookie jar.
  (hold up one finger)
Who me?
  (point to self)
Yes you.
  (point to group)
Couldn't be.
  (shake head)
Then who?
  (shrug, hands turned up)

  *(repeat five times, holding up an
  additional finger each time)*

ACTION RHYME

Two Little Apples

Way, way up in an apple tree
  (stretch hands overhead)
Two little apples smiled at me.
  (clench fist to represent apples)
I shook that tree as hard as I could,
  (shake body)
Down came those apples—
  (put fists on the floor)
Ummmmm, they were good!
  (rub stomach)

FLANNEL BOARD POEM

I Eat My Peas with Honey

I eat my peas with honey.
I've done it all my life.
I know it may seem funny.
But it keeps them on my knife.

Directions

Enlarge the patterns on a photocopier to a size appropriate for your
flannel board.

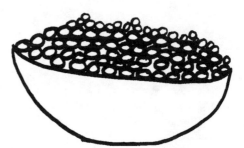

STORY WITH VISUALS

The Cat Who Was Such a Glutton

This story can be found in
Norwegian Folk Tales, by Peter
Christen Asbornsen, on page 161.
Another version of this
story is *The Fat Cat*
by Jack Kent.

Directions

Use a photocopier to enlarge the cat
pattern onto a transparency. Project
the image (to about three feet tall)
so that it is large enough to slide the
other figures into its mouth. Trace it

onto a large piece of poster board or foam board. Cut out the image and add color with markers or paint. Tape clear plastic over the stomach area. Attach a piece of poster board to the back of the cat to form an envelope to catch the items that are dropped into the stomach through the mouth. Tape the poster board securely around the bottom and sides of the transparent stomach so the items do not slip out. Photocopy, color, cut out, and laminate the items that the cat eats. Use the pattern for the woman on page 78, the man on page 119, and the cow on page 120. This story can also be adapted for the flannel board.

SONG

Peanut on a Railroad Track

  C   F   C
A peanut sat on the railroad track,

                  C
Its heart was all a-flutter.

                        F   C
A train came chugging down the track,

  G   C
Ooops! Peanut Butter!

VIDEO

Show *Frog Goes to Dinner* from Phoenix/BFA Films (12 minutes).

CRAFT

Make a Meal

Supply the children with pictures of food cut from magazines. Let them glue the pictures onto paper plates to create their own delicious meals.

Supplies

paper plates
magazines
glue

Just Plain Silly

PUBLICITY

"I saw you in the street, I saw you in a tree, I saw you in the bathtub—
Whoops! Pardon me!" Join us at the _____
Library on _____ for some silly songs, funny stories, a short
video, and an amusing craft activity. Call _____ to register.
Preschoolers, ages 3–6.

BOOK SUGGESTIONS

Denim, Sue. *The Dumb Bunnies.*

Lester, Helen. *The Revenge of the
    Magic Chicken.*

Numeroff, Laura. *Chimps Don't Wear
    Glasses.*

Riddell, Chris. *When the Walrus
    Comes.*

Wieser, David. *Tuesday.*

Willis, Jeanne. *Earthlets, As
    Explained by Professor Xargle.*

Wood, Audrey. *Silly Sally.*

160

ACTION RHYME

Clap! Stamp! Shake!

You can clap your hands.
  (clap, clap, clap)
You can clap your hands.
  (clap, clap, clap)
When the day is done and you want
  some fun,
You can clap your hands.
  (clap, clap, clap)

You can stamp your feet
  (stamp, stamp, stamp)
You can stamp your feet
  (stamp, stamp, stamp)
When the day is done and you want
  some fun,
You can stamp your feet,
  (stamp, stamp, stamp)
And you can clap your hands.
  (clap, clap, clap)

You can shake your head,
  (shake, shake, shake)
You can shake your head,
  (shake, shake, shake)
When the day is done and you want
  some fun,
You can shake your head,
  (shake, shake, shake)
And you can stamp your feet,
  (stamp, stamp, stamp)
And you can clap your hands.
  (clap, clap, clap)

You can make a noise.
  (waah, waah, waah)
You can make a noise.
  (waah, waah, waah)
When the day is done and you want
  some fun,
You can make a noise,
  (waah, waah, waah)
And you can shake your head,
  (shake, shake, shake)
And you can stamp your feet,
  (stamp, stamp, stamp)
And you can clap your hands.
  (clap, clap, clap)

You can do all four.
  (everything together 3 times)
You can do all four.
  (everything together 3 times)

When the day is done and you want
  some fun,
You can do all four.
  (everything together 3 times)

SONG

Do Your Ears Hang Low?

Do your ears hang low?
Do they wobble to and fro?
  (suit actions to words)
Can you tie them in a knot?
Can you tie them in a bow?
Can you throw them over your
  shoulder
Like a Continental soldier?
Do your ears hang low?

FINGER PUPPETS

Little Clown

This little clown is fat and gay.
This little clown does tricks all day.
This little clown is tall and strong.
This little clown sings a funny song.
This little clown is wee and small.
But he can do anything at all.

Directions

Use the pattern to make clowns
out of felt or poster board.
Attach Velcro to the back of
each clown and to the fingers
of a glove.

FLANNEL BOARD SONG

Aiken Drum

There was a man lived in the moon,
In the moon, in the moon,
There was a man lived in the moon,
And his name was Aiken Drum.

And he played upon a ladle,
A ladle, a ladle,
He played upon a ladle,
And his name was Aiken Drum.

And his hair was made of string
    beans . . .

And his eyes were made of gum
    drops . . .

And his nose was a banana . . .

And his mouth was made of
    watermelon . . .

And he played upon a ladle . . .

There was a man lived in the
    moon . . .

—Scottish Nursery Song
adapted by Diane Briggs

Directions

Enlarge the patterns on a
photocopier to the desired
size for your flannel board.
Make multiple string bean
pieces for the hair. As you
sing the song, add the hair,
eyes, nose, and mouth.
For tips on making story
figures, see the section on
flannel board storytelling in
the introduction.

VIDEO

Show *I Know an Old Lady Who Swallowed a Fly* from International Film Bureau (9 minutes).

CRAFT

Create a Silly Animal

Before the program, cut pictures of animals out of old magazines. Cut the pictures up so you have a variety of animal heads, bodies, legs, and tails. Mix the pieces together in a container. Now let the children assemble unique animals using the cut up parts. They can glue the animals onto a construction paper background.

Supplies

construction paper
magazines
glue

Monster Mash

PUBLICITY

What did the little monster say to the big monster? "I want my mummy!"

Get ready for a monstrously good time at the _____

Library on _____. Enjoy stories, songs, and monster dancing.

Call _____ to register. Preschoolers, ages 3–6.

BOOK SUGGESTIONS

Bunting, Eve. *Ghost's Hour, Spook's Hour.*

Clarke, Gus. *Ten Green Monsters.*

Emberly, Ed. *Go Away, Big Green Monster!*

Hutchins, Pat. *Silly Billy.*

Mayer, Mercer. *There's Something in My Attic.*

Meddaugh, Susan. *Too Many Monsters.*

Paraskevas, Betty. *Monster Beach.*

FINGER PLAYS

This Little Monster

This little monster went to market,
This little monster stayed home,
This little monster had roast beef,
This little monster had none,
And this little monster cried, "Boo,
    hoo, hoo"
All the way home.

You may do this as a finger play
or perform the rhyme with finger
puppets by using the pattern to
make five monsters out of felt or
poster board. Attach them to the fingers of a glove with Velcro.

Scary Eyes

See my big and scary eyes?
    (circle fingers around eyes)
Look out now, a big surprise.
Boo!!!!
    (quickly remove fingers)

POEM WITH VISUAL ENHANCEMENT

The Monster's Lunch

This monster can eat a hearty lunch.
Among his favorites to munch and
    crunch
Are alligator eyeballs, armadillos,
    and bears.
He also adores anaconda in a lus-
    cious sauce of pears.
If his stomach still grumbles,
He'll eat a moose,
And perhaps consume a hog, mud
    turtle, or goose.

But when he's depressed,
Chocolate-covered tarantulas are
    best.

He enjoys bats because they're
    chewy,
And slimy slugs are nice and gooey,
And wolverines make a feisty
    foodstuff.
When you think he's had enough,
He can still consume a whale,
Ingest an ox's tail,
And nibble on a hedgehog or two.

When he is finally through,
With nothing left to chew,
He goes off to sleep,
To dream of sheep,
And mint-green jelly,
And other things to put in his belly.

Directions

Enlarge the monster pattern on a photocopier and trace it onto a transparency. Project the image so that its mouth is large enough to "eat" the other animals (about three feet tall). Trace it onto a large piece of poster board or foam board.

Add color with markers or paint and cut out the monster. Tape clear plastic over the stomach area. Attach a piece of poster board to the back of the body to form an envelope to catch the items that are dropped into the stomach through the mouth.

cut out

cut out

Tape poster board securely around the bottom and sides so the items do not slip out. Photocopy (enlarge slightly), color, cut out, and laminate the items that the monster eats. Tape the poem to the back of the body for easy reference.

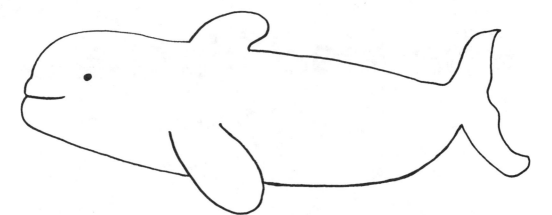

ACTION RHYME

Monster, Monster

Monster, monster, turn around.
   (suit actions to words)
Monster, monster, touch the ground.
Monster, monster, reach up high.
Monster, monster, bug out your eyes.
Monster, monster, bend your knees.
Monster, monster, growl and sneeze.
Monster, monster, climb into bed.
Monster, monster, rest your head.

SONG

I'm Bringing Home a Baby Purple Monster

(*Tune:* I'm Bringing Home a Baby Bumblebee)

I'm bringing home a baby purple
   monster,
   *(cup hands together as if holding
      something small)*
Won't my mommy think it's a
   disaster,
'Cause I'm bringing home a baby
   purple monster.
   (peek into cupped hands)
Ahhhh!!! He scared me!

ACTIVITY

Dance the Monster Mash

Find a recording of the song "Monster Mash" and play it while doing a monster dance.

VIDEO

Show *Where the Wild Things Are* from Weston Woods (8 minutes).

CRAFT

Pet Monster

Invite children to glue small pieces of craft fur onto a precut egg carton section. They can add googly eyes and precut felt arms.

Supplies

craft fur in assorted colors
egg carton sections
felt
googly eyes
glue

The Mad Hatter's Tea Party

PUBLICITY

Join Alice and all her friends from Wonderland at the _____

Library on _____. Bring a half dozen cookies to share, and

we'll have a tea party! Call _____ to register. Preschoolers,

ages 3–6.

BOOK SUGGESTIONS

De Regniers, Beatrice Schenk. *May I Bring a Friend?*

Guthrie, Donna. *Mrs. Gigglebelly Is Coming for Tea.*

Numeroff, Laura Joffe. *If You Give a Mouse a Cookie.*

SKIT

Perform this skit to introduce the program. If you don't have enough staff, consider enlisting some volunteers. Be sure to be in costume: Alice with long blond hair and a pinafore; Rabbit with vest, pocket watch, tail, and ears; Hatter with large hat, vest, and pants.

A Mad Tea Party

(Courtesy of Bethlehem Public Library)

Setting: A tea table is set up at the front of the room. The Mad Hatter and the White Rabbit are seated, drinking tea, at one end of the table. There is an empty arm chair at the other end.

Alice enters. Mad Hatter and White Rabbit: No room! No room!

Alice: *(indignantly)* There's plenty of room! *(sits down in the armchair)*

Rabbit: Have some lemonade.

Alice: *(looks around)* I don't see any lemonade.

Rabbit: There isn't any. *(Rabbit and Hatter look at each other and laugh.)*

Alice: *(angrily)* Then it wasn't very polite of you to offer it!

Rabbit: *(shrugs)* It wasn't very polite of you to sit down without being invited.

Alice: I didn't know it was YOUR table. There's an extra chair.

Hatter: *(to Alice)* You really need a haircut.

Alice: *(severely)* You should learn not to make personal remarks. It's very rude.

Hatter: *(ignores this)* What do you get when you put a bunch of ducks together in a box?

Alice: *(thinking)* I don't know.

Hatter: A box of quackers!

(Hatter and Rabbit laugh uproariously. Alice looks disgusted.)

Rabbit: How can you tell when an elephant has been in your refrigerator?

Alice: I don't know.

Rabbit: By the footprints in the butter!

(All laugh.)

Hatter: *(takes a watch out of her pocket, looks at it, shakes it, holds it to her ear)* What day of the month is it?

Alice: It's the eleventh of March.

Hatter: *(sighs)* Two days wrong! *(glares at Rabbit)* I TOLD you not to put butter in it!

Rabbit: *(meekly)* It was the BEST butter.

Hatter: *(grumbling)* Yes, but some crumbs must have got in as well. You shouldn't have put it in with the bread knife.

Rabbit: *(takes the watch, looks at it gloomily, dips it into her cup of tea, holds it to her ear)* It WAS the best butter, you know.

Alice: *(staring)* What a funny watch! It tells the day of the month, but not the time!

(Hatter and Rabbit look at each other, puzzled, then turn to stare at Alice.)

Hatter: Why should it tell time?

Alice: *(sighs and shakes her head)* I don't understand.

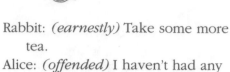

Rabbit: *(earnestly)* Take some more tea.

Alice: *(offended)* I haven't had any yet, so I can't take more.

Hatter: You mean you can't take less. It's very easy to take more than nothing.

Alice: *(annoyed)* Nobody asked your opinion.

Hatter: *(triumphantly)* Now who's making personal remarks?

Alice: *(stands up, disgusted)* I'm never coming here again! This is the most ridiculous tea party I've ever been to in all my life! *(exits)*

Hatter: Oh, come on! This can't be the MOST ridiculous one you've ever been to!

Hatter and Rabbit: *(rise and follow Alice out, bantering back and forth)* Do you think this is the most ridiculous tea party? No, it can't be! *(etc.)*

—*adapted by* Lisa Bouchard

FINGER PLAY

Here's a Cup

Here's a cup, and here's a cup
   (cup both hands to represent cups)
And here's a pot of tea
   (make a fist and extend thumb to represent spout)
Pour a cup, and pour a cup,
   (do pouring motion)
And have a cup with me.
   (pretend to drink from cup)

ACTION RHYME/SONG

I'm a Little Teapot

I'm a little teapot
Short and stout.
Here is my handle,
   (put one hand on hip)
Here is my spout.
   (hold out other arm in the shape of a spout)
When I get all steamed up,
Then I shout,
Just tip me over,
   (tip body to one side)
And pour me out.

ACTIVITY

Tea Party

Set up tables with real cups and saucers, tablecloths, centerpieces, and plates for the cookies. Alice should go around with an attractive teapot and serve everyone tea. Apple juice may be substituted for tea.

VIDEO

Cue up to the tea party scene in Disney's *Alice in Wonderland*. This segment lasts about 10 minutes.

It's Raining, It's Pouring

PUBLICITY

Do you love to run in the rain and jump in all the puddles? Then you'll love our storytime on _____ at the _____ Library. We'll have rain stories, rain songs, a short video, and a rainbow craft. Call _____ to register. Preschoolers, ages 3–6.

BOOK SUGGESTIONS

Carlson, Nancy. *What If It Never Stops Raining?*

Cooney, Nancy Evans. *The Umbrella Day.*

Ehlert, Lois. *Planting a Rainbow.*

Ginsburg, Mirra. *Mushroom in the Rain.*

Hoban, Julia. *Amy Loves the Rain.*

Holl, Adelaide. *The Rain Puddle.*

Sturges, Philemon. *Rainsong/Snowsong.*

Wood, Audrey. *The Napping House.*

173

FINGER PLAYS

Raindrops

Ten little raindrops, dancing on the
walk.
(tap fingers on floor)
Pitter patter, pitter patter, that's the
way they talk.
Out comes the yellow sun, shining
in the sky,
(make a large circle with fingers)
And away all the raindrops fly,
fly, fly.
*(fingers hurry away behind
back)*

Pitter Patter

Pitter, patter falls the rain,
(flutter fingers down)
On the roof and window pane.
*(touch fingers together overhead
for roof, pretend to press against
window with palms)*
Softly, softly, it comes down,
(flutter fingers down)
And makes a stream that runs
around.
*(make a winding motion with
fingers)*
Flowers lift their heads and say:
(cup hands and stretch arms up)
"A nice cool drink for us today."

FINGER PLAY/SONG

Eensy-Weensy Spider

Eensy-weensy spider went up the
water spout.
(wiggle fingers upward)
Down came the rain and washed the
spider out.
*(flutter fingers down, sweep arms
outward)*
Out came the sun and dried up all
the rain,
(circle arms overhead)
And the eensy-weensy spider went
up the spout again.
(wiggle fingers upward)

SONG

It's Raining, It's Pouring

It's raining, it's pouring,
The old man is snoring.
He bumped his head
And he went to bed
And he couldn't get up in the
morning.

FLANNEL BOARD STORY

My Red Umbrella

My Red Umbrella by Robert Bright is a story about a little girl who provides shelter under her umbrella for a menagerie of animals. The book is quite small and is difficult to share in a group setting, but when it is adapted for the flannel board, it's delightful. When telling the story with the flannel board, be sure to show the book and explain that it may be borrowed from the library.

Directions

Enlarge the patterns on a photocopier to the size appropriate for your flannel board. (The umbrella should be especially large.) For tips on making story figures see the section on flannel board storytelling in the introduction.

VIDEO

Show *Incy, Wincy Spider* from Direct Cinema (5 minutes).

CRAFT

Rainbow Window Decoration

Precut rainbow shapes out of poster board and draw two semicircles on them. Let children color their rainbows and help them add multicolored glitter. They can glue cotton clouds to the ends. When they are finished, punch a hole in the top for them and tie on a string. Suggest that they hang their rainbows in a window at home.

Supplies

cotton or stuffing
poster board
crayons
washable markers
glitter
string
glue
hole punch

Mr. Sun

PUBLICITY

Join us at the _____ Library on _____
for some stories, songs, and finger plays to warm you up for spring. See a
short video and make your own sun visor to take home. Call _____
to register. Preschoolers, ages 3–6.

BOOK SUGGESTIONS

Caple, Kathy. *The Coolest Place in Town*.

Dowling, Paul. *Jimmy's Sunny Book*.

Ginsburg, Mirra. *Where Does the Sun Go at Night?*

Hill, Eric. *Spot Goes to the Beach*.

Hoban, Julia. *Amy Loves the Sun*.

Marzollo, Jean. *Sun Song*.

Novak, Matt. *Claude and Sun*.

FINGER PLAY

A Little Boy Went Walking

A little boy went walking
    (walk two fingers)
One lovely summer day.
He saw a little rabbit
    (hold up two fingers)
That quickly ran away.
    (hop fingers behind back)
He saw the shining river
    (make wavy motions with hands)
Go winding in and out.
And little fishes in it
    (wiggle index fingers)
Were playing all about.

—Emilie Poulsson

ACTION RHYME

Spring Sun, Spring Showers

During spring it often showers,
    (flutter fingers)
Or the sun shines for many hours.
    (arms form circle overhead)
Both are good for flowers.
    (cup hands and extend arms
      upward)

SONG

Mr. Sun

              G
Oh, Mister Sun, Sun,

 A7
Mister Golden Sun,

    D7   G
Please shine down on me.

              G
Oh, Mister Sun, Sun,

 A7
Mister Golden Sun,

 D7
Hiding behind a tree.

      G   D
These little children are asking you

        G
To please come out

            D
So we can play with you.

              G
Oh, Mister Sun, Sun,

 A7
Mister Golden Sun,

    D7   G
Please shine down on me.

FLANNEL BOARD STORY

How Grandmother Spider Stole the Sun

See page 50 for directions and story patterns.

VIDEO

Show *The Little Rooster Who Made the Sun Rise* from Coronet Films (11 minutes).

CRAFT

Sun Visor

Precut visors out of poster board and punch holes in both sides of the visor. Tie a piece of elastic to the holes. Let the children decorate the visors with stickers, glitter, pom-poms, or other materials you have on hand.

Supplies

poster board
stickers
pom-poms
glitter
elastic
glue

Stories with Grandma and Grandpa

PUBLICITY

Grandparents or honorary grandparents and grandchildren are invited to join us at the _____ Library for some wonderful stories, songs, and fun activities. Work together and create a memory book to take home. Call _____ to register. Preschoolers, ages 3–6.

BOOK SUGGESTIONS

Beil, Karen. *Grandma According to Me.*

Buckley, Helen. *Grandfather and I.*

————. *Grandmother and I.*

Daly, Niki. *Not So Fast, Songololo.*

Dexter, Alison. *Grandma.*

Greenfield, Eloise. *Grandpa's Face.*

McKean, Thomas. *Hooray for Grandma Jo!*

FINGER PLAYS

Open and Shut Them

Open and shut them, open and shut
  them,
  (open and shut hands)
And give a little clap.
Open and shut them, open and shut
  them,
And put them in your lap.

Creep them, creep them, creep
  them, creep them,
  (creep fingers up front of body)
Right up to your chin.
Open up your little mouth,
  (open mouth)
But do not let them in!
  *(quickly hide hands behind
  back)*

Grandma's Glasses

Here are Grandma's glasses.
  (fingers circle eyes)
Here is Grandma's hat.
  (place imaginary hat on head)
This is the way
She folds her hands
  (fold hands)
And lays them in her lap.
  (put hands in lap)

Here are Grandpa's glasses.
  (fingers circle eyes)
Here is Grandpa's hat.
  (place imaginary hat on head)
This is the way he folds his arms
  (fold arms)
Just like that.

SONG

Special Grandma and Grandpa

(*Tune:* Oscar Mayer "I Wish I Were an Oscar Mayer Wiener" theme song)

  C   D7
Have you ever seen such a special Grandma?
     G   C G
She plays with me and loves me all the time.
          C   D7
Have you ever seen such a special Grandma?
   G   C
I sure am very happy that she's mine.

    C   D7
Have you ever seen such a special Grandpa?
     G   C G
He plays with me and loves me all the time.
         C   D7
Have you ever seen such a special Grandpa?
   G   C
I sure am very happy that he's mine.

FLANNEL BOARD STORY

The Enormous Turnip

Enlarge the patterns on a photocopier to a size appropriate for your
flannel board. For tips on making
story figures check the section on
flannel board storytelling in the
introduction.

There are several versions of this
story that can be found in collections
of Russian folktales or in picture
book format. One good source is
The Turnip by Pierr Morgan.

When telling the story, the turnip
should be covered with a piece
of brown felt. At the end of the
story "pull" the turnip up.

VIDEO

Show *The Napping House* from Weston Woods (5 minutes).

CRAFT

Memory Book

Ask the program participants to bring in a few snapshots, cards, drawings, or other mementos they would like to put in a memory book. Provide each grandparent and preschooler group with a book into which they can glue the mementos. To make the books, use ten or twelve sheets of quality paper. Wallpaper or light poster board may be used for covers. Punch holes in the edges and tie them with ribbon. Let the children draw pictures in the book too.

Supplies

wallpaper or light poster board for covers
hole punch
ribbon
paper
glue

Delightful Dolls

PUBLICITY

Bring your favorite dolly to the _____ Library on
_____ and enjoy doll stories, poems, songs, and activities.
Create a new doll to take home. Please call _____ to register.
Preschoolers, ages 3–6.

BOOK SUGGESTIONS

Bang, Molly. *One Fall Day.*

Berger, Barbara Helen. *The Jewel Heart.*

Conrad, Pam. *Doll Face Has a Party!*

———. *The Tub People.*

Hutchins, Pat. *Changes, Changes.*

Polacco, Patricia. *Babushka's Doll.*

Waddell, Martin. *The Toymaker.*

Wells, Rosemary. *Peabody.*

Wright, Dare. *The Lonely Doll.*

FINGER PUPPETS

This Little Doll

This little doll is dressed in red.
This little doll has a hat on her head.
This little doll can cry and talk.
This little doll can crawl and walk.
This little doll is tiny and small.
But she's the one I love best of all.

Directions

Use the patterns to make five doll
figures with felt or posterboard.
Attach them to the fingers of a glove
with Velcro.

ACTION RHYMES

Miss Polly Had a Dolly

Miss Polly had a dolly
Who was sick, sick, sick,
  (make a rocking motion with
    arms)
So she phoned the doctor
To come quick, quick, quick.
  (pretend to dial phone)

The doctor came
With his bag and hat,
  (swing arms as if holding a
    doctor's bag)
And he knocked on the door
With a rat-tat-tat.
  (pretend to knock)

He looked at the dolly,
And he shook his head;
  (shake head)
Then he said, "Miss Polly,
Put her straight to bed."
  (shake finger)

He wrote on a paper
For a pill, pill, pill,
  (write on palm)
"I'll be back in the morning
With my bill, bill, bill."
  (wave good-bye)

Rag Doll

Let's play rag doll.
  (suit actions to words)
Let's not make a sound.
Fling your arms and body
Loosely around.
Fling your arms and your feet
And let your head go free,
Be the raggediest rag doll
You ever did see.

VIDEO

Show *Matrioska* from Contemporary Films (5 minutes).

CRAFT

Clothespin Doll

Provide the children with straight clothespins and wooden bases to stand them in. These are available in most craft stores. Let children glue small pieces of fabric or felt to the clothespins for clothes and use markers to draw faces. Yarn or craft hair may be glued on the head. Give the children precut felt arms to glue onto their dolls.

Supplies

yarn or craft hair
washable markers
felt and fabric
wooden bases
clothespins
glue
precut felt arms

Hats Off to You!

PUBLICITY

Preschoolers, wear your favorite hats to the _____
Library on _____. We will have stories about hats, hat songs,
and a short video. Create a new hat to take home. Call _____
to register.

BOOK SUGGESTIONS

Gill, Madelaine. *The Spring Hat.*

Miller, Margaret. *Whose Hat?*

Nodset, Joan L. *Who Took the Farmer's Hat?*

Slobodkina, Esphyr. *Caps for Sale.*

Smax, William. *Big Pig's Hat.*

Smith, William Jay. *Ho for a Hat!*

Van Laan, Nancy. *This Is the Hat: A Story in Rhyme.*

FLANNEL BOARD POEM

Magic Hat

Here's my magic hat.
Presto! I'm pulling out a bird that's
   white.
It's flapping its wings, getting ready
   to take flight.
Shazam! I'm pulling out a kitten
   that's yellow.
Let me pet you softly, you little furry
   fellow.
Hocus-pocus! Out jumps a frog that's
   green.
With the googliest eyes I ever have
   seen.
Poof! Here's a tiny monster with
   eyes that are yellow.
Better watch out for that little fellow.
Abracadabra! What will come out
   now?
Mooo! I declare! It's a big brown cow!
Alacazam! Here's something furry,
   soft, and white.
Could it be a rabbit? Yes, you're
   right.

Directions

Enlarge the patterns on a photocopier to a size appropriate for your
flannel board. Use the cow pattern
on page 120.

For tips on making story figures
see the section on flannel board
storytelling in the introduction.

Place the hat on the flannel
board. Conceal each item in your
hand as you move it near the hat.
Pretend to pull each item out of the
hat, then put it on the flannel board.

ACTION RHYME

Hats, Hats, Hats

A clown wears a funny hat that's
    pointed at the top.
    (hands form point on head)
A firefighter's hat protects her as she
    makes a fire stop.
    (circle head with hands)
A baseball player needs his hat
    when sun gets in his eyes.
    (indicate a visor)
An astronaut needs a helmet when
    into space she flies.
    *(place imaginary helmet on
    head)*
A cowboy rides a bronco and wears
    a wide-brimmed hat.
    (hands encircle head)
But when the bronco bucks him off,
    his hat may end up flat.
    *(palms together to indicate
    flatness)*

SONG

Mary Wore Her Red Hat

(*Adapted from* "Mary Wore Her Red
Dress")

  G   D   G
Mary wore her red hat, red hat, red hat
  G   D   G
Mary wore her red hat all day long.

Thomas wore his blue hat . . .
Brian wore his green hat . . .
Jessica wore her pink hat . . .
Sarah wore her yellow hat . . .

(*Note:* If possible use the names of
the children in your story program
as you sing this song.)

VIDEO

Show "The Hat" by Toni Ungerer,
found on the video *Dr. De Soto and
Other Stories* from Children's Circle
(7 minutes).

CRAFT

Make a Hat

Staple poster board visors onto
paper bowls. Let the children decorate their hats with craft feathers,
pom-poms, sequins, glitter, or fabric
scraps. If needed, attach yarn or
elastic to the sides of the hats to
help keep them on.

Supplies

stapler
craft feathers
pom-poms
sequins
fabric scraps
glitter
paper bowls
yarn
elastic
glue

In Our Garden

PUBLICITY

Delight in stories and songs about things that grow at the
_____ Library on _____. We will also have time
to plant some seeds. Call _____ to register. Preschoolers,
ages 3–6.

BOOK SUGGESTIONS

Bunting, Eve. *Sunflower House*.

Krauss, Ruth. *The Carrot Seed*.

Mallett, David. *Inch by Inch: The Garden Song*.

Morgan, Pierr. *The Turnip*.

Stevens, Janet. *Tops and Bottoms*.

Westcott, Nadine. *The Giant Vegetable Garden*.

FINGER PLAYS

My Garden

This is my garden,
(one hand out palm up)
I'll rake it with care,
(rake palms with fingers)
And then some flower seeds
(sprinkle seeds)
I'll plant in there.
(pat palm with fingers)

The sun will shine,
(circle arms overhead)
And the rain will fall,
(wiggle fingers downward)
And my garden will blossom,
(make fists, open fingers slowly)
Growing straight and tall.
(reach hands high overhead)

Five Plump Peas

Five plump peas in a peapod
    pressed.
    (press two fists together)
One grew, two grew, so did all the
    rest.
    *(have fingers gradually pop up
    from fist)*
They grew and they grew and did
    not stop.
    (slowly move hands apart)
Until one day the pod went pop!
    *(bring hands together with a big
    clap)*

A Little Plant

In the heart of a seed,
    (make a fist to represent seed)
Buried down so deep,
A little plant lay fast asleep.

"Awake," said the sun,
    (circle arms overhead)
"Come up through the earth."
"Awake" said the rain,
    (flutter fingers downward)
"We are giving you birth."

The little plant heard
With a happy sigh,
And pointed its petals
    (open hand and turn up fingers)
Up to the sky.
    (raise hand to indicate growth)

SONG

The Garden Song

"The Garden Song" can be found in the book *Inch by Inch: The Garden Song* by David Mallett and on the album *Peter, Paul, and Mommy Too.*

FLANNEL BOARD STORY

The Enormous Turnip

The instructions and patterns for this story can be found on pages 183–4.

VIDEO

Show "The Garden" from *Frog and Toad Together* from Churchill (7 minutes).

CRAFT

Green-Haired Guy

Give each child a Styrofoam cup filled with soil. Draw funny faces on the cups and sprinkle on grass seed. Tell children to take their cups home, add sunlight and water, and watch for some green hair to sprout.

Once upon a Fairytale

PUBLICITY

Enter a land of enchantment at the _____
Library on _____. Enjoy hearing stories about princesses,
princes, dragons, and more. Make a shiny dragon to take home. Call
_____ to register. Preschoolers, ages 3–6.

BOOK SUGGESTIONS

Brett, Jan. *Goldilocks and the Three Bears*.

Cauley, Lorinda Bryan. *Jack and the Beanstalk*.

Cole, Babette. *Prince Cinders*.

Galdone, Paul. *The Three Billy Goats Gruff*.

Hilton, Nette. *Prince Lachlan*.

Inkpen, Mick. *Lullabyhullaballoo*.

Little, Jack. *Once upon a Golden Apple*.

Munsch, Robert. *The Paper Bag Princess*.

Thayer, Jane. *The Popcorn Dragon*.

SONG

Sing a Song of Sixpence

  C
Sing a song of sixpence

  G7
A pocket full of rye,

Four and twenty blackbirds

  C
Baked in a pie.

  C
When the pie was opened,

   G7
The birds began to sing;

 G7
Wasn't that a dainty dish

        C
To set before a king?

    C
The king was in the counting house,

  G7
Counting all his money;

The queen was in the parlor,

 C
Eating bread and honey.

   C
The maid was in the garden,

    G7
Hanging out the clothes,

   G7
When along came a blackbird,

       C
And nipped off her nose.

       —Mother Goose

FINGER PLAY

Two Little Fairies

Two little fairies sitting on my
    window sill,
    (hold up index fingers)
One named Jack, one named Jill.
Fly away Jack, fly away Jill.
    (flutter hands behind back)
Come back Jack, come back Jill.
    (bring fingers back)
Two little fairies sitting on my
    window sill.

FLANNEL BOARD STORY

The Frog Prince

Enlarge the patterns on a photocopier to the appropriate size and make the story figures out of felt. For tips on making story figures, see the section on flannel board storytelling in the introduction.

    Memorize a simplified version of the story, such as Paul Galdone's, and practice telling it with the story

figures before you do the storytime. The frog should be hidden under the well when it is placed on the flannel board. Pull the frog out of the well when he talks to the princess. When he eats off her plate, put him on the table. At the end of the story, quickly snatch him off the flannel board and replace him with the prince.

table

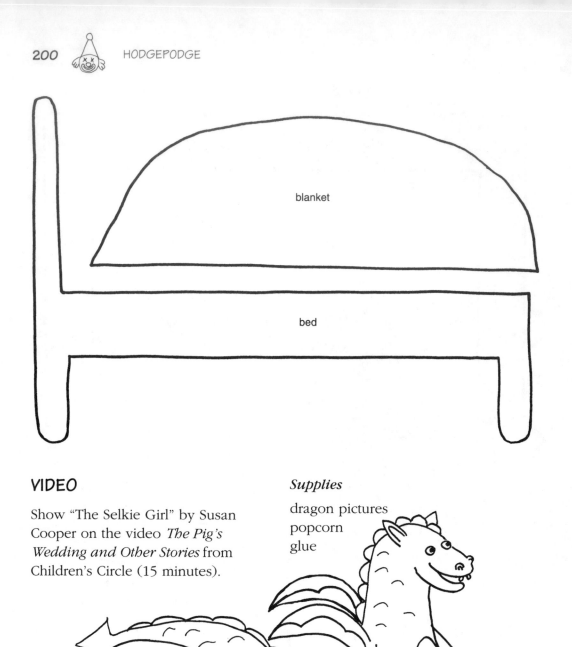

blanket

bed

VIDEO

Show "The Selkie Girl" by Susan Cooper on the video *The Pig's Wedding and Other Stories* from Children's Circle (15 minutes).

CRAFT

Dragon

Make enlarged photocopies of the dragon picture. Let the children glue on shiny "scales" of commercially available shiny confetti (which can be purchased from craft or party stores). If you like, let them glue on popcorn to make the popcorn dragon. Add silver or gold glitter to the wings.

Supplies

dragon pictures
popcorn
glue

Bedtime Stories

PUBLICITY

Jump into your pj's, bring your blanket and teddy, and come to the
_____ Library on _____ to enjoy bed-
time stories, songs, and finger plays. Call _____ to register.
Preschoolers, ages 3–6.

BOOK SUGGESTIONS

Baker, Alan. *Goodnight William.*

Brown, Margaret Wise. *Goodnight Moon.*

Dale, Penny. *Ten out of Bed.*

Duke, Kate. *Bedtime.*

Field, Eugene. *Wynken, Blynken, and Nod.*

Fox, Mem. *Time for Bed.*

Ginsburg, Mirra. *Asleep, Asleep.*

Horwitz, Elinor. *When the Sky Is Like Lace.*

Nightingale, Sandy. *A Giraffe on the Moon.*

FINGER PLAY

This Little Boy

This little boy is ready for bed,
    (hold up index finger)
Down on the pillow he puts his
    head,
    (lay index finger in palm of
      other hand)
Wraps himself in the cover tight,
    (wrap fingers around "boy")
And here he sleeps all the night.
    (rock hands)

When mommy comes, he opens
    his eyes,
    (open hand)
And back with a toss the cover flies,
Up he jumps, is dressed and away,
    (index finger jumps up, pretend
      to put clothes on finger)
Ready to work and play all day.
    (wiggle finger)

ACTION RHYME

Good Night

Two little hands go clap, clap, clap,
    (suit action to words)
Two little arms lie in my lap,
Two little feet go bump, bump,
    bump,
Two little legs give one big jump,
Two little eyes are shut up tight,
One little voice whispers low,
    "Good night."
    (cradle head on hands)

SONG

All the Pretty Little Horses

Dm   Gm
Hush-a-bye, don't you cry,

Am   A   Dm
Go to sleepy little baby.

Dm   Gm
When you wake, you shall have

Am   A   Dm
All the pretty little horses.

Dm   Gm
Blacks and bays, dapples and grays,

Am   A   Dm
Coach and six-a-little horses.

Dm   Gm
Mommy loves, and Daddy loves,

Am   A   Dm
And mommy loves her little baby.

Dm   Gm
Go to sleep, go to sleep,

Am   A   Dm
Go to sleep you little baby.

FLANNEL BOARD SONG

Five Teddies in the Bed

(*Tune:* "Ten in the Bed")

There were five teddies in the bed,
And the little one said, "Roll over,
   roll over."
So they all rolled over, and one fell
   out.

   (*repeat with* 4, 3, 2, *and* 1)

And the little one said, "GOOD-
NIGHT!"

Directions

Enlarge the patterns on a photocopier to the size appropriate for
your flannel board. For tips on
making story figures see the section
on flannel board storytelling in the
introduction.

Make four

Make one

VIDEO

Show *The Napping House* from Weston Woods (5 minutes).

CRAFT

Dress Teddy for Bed

Enlarge the teddy bear and night clothes on a photocopier. (Make one set for each child.) Before the program, cut out the pajamas. Let children color the teddy and clothes. Then suggest they get their teddy ready for bed by gluing on its night clothes.

Supplies

paper
glue
crayons

BIBLIOGRAPHY

Aardema, Verna. *Borreguita and the Coyote*. New York: Knopf, 1991.

———. *Why Mosquitos Buzz in People's Ears*. New York: Dial, 1975.

Aatley, Judy. *When One Cat Woke Up*. New York: Dial, 1990.

Accorsi, William. *Friendship's First Thanksgiving*. New York: Holiday, 1992.

Alexander, Sue. *There's More . . . Much More*. San Diego: Gulliver, 1987.

Allen, Pamela. *Belinda*. New York: Viking, 1992.

———. *My Cat Maisey*. New York: Viking, 1990.

Andrews, Sylvia. *Rattlebone Rock*. New York: HarperCollins, 1995.

Arbuthnot, May Hill. *The Arbuthnot Anthology of Children's Literature*. Chicago: Scott Foresman, 1961.

Argent, Kerry. *Happy Birthday, Wombat!* Boston: Little, Brown, 1989.

———. *Wombat and Bandicoot: Best of Friends*. Boston: Little, Brown, 1988.

Arnold, Ted. *Green Wilma*. New York: Dial, 1993.

Arnott, Kathleen. *Spiders, Crabs, and Creepy Crawlers: Two African Folktales*. Champaign, Ill.: Garrard, 1978.

Asbornsen, Peter Christen. *Norwegian Folk Tales*. New York: Viking, 1960.

Asch, Frank. *Just Like Daddy*. New York: Simon & Schuster, 1981.

———. *Mooncake*. Englewood Cliffs, N.J.: Prentice-Hall, 1983.

Ata Te. *Baby Rattlesnake*. San Francisco: Children's, 1989.

Baker, Alan. *Benjamin's Balloon*. New York: Lothrop, Lee & Shepard, 1990.

———. *Goodnight William*. Hagerstone, Md.: Deutsch, 1990.

Balian, Laura. *A Garden for a Groundhog*. Nashville: Abingdon, 1985.

Bang, Molly. *One Fall Day*. New York: Greenwillow, 1994.

Barrett, Judi. *Cloudy with a Chance of Meatballs*. New York: Aladdin, 1978.

Barton, Byron. *I Want to Be an Astronaut*. New York: Crowell, 1988.

Beil, Karen. *Grandma According to Me*. New York: Doubleday, 1992.

Bender, Robert. *A Most Unusual Lunch*. New York: Dial, 1994.

———. *A Little Witch Magic*. New York: H. Holt, 1992.

Berger, Barbara Helen. *The Jewel Heart*. New York: Philomel, 1994.

Birney, Betty G. *Tyrannosaurus Tex*. Boston: Houghton Mifflin, 1994.

Blumenthal, Nancy. *Count-A-Saurus*. Four Winds, 1989.

Bodsworth, Nan. *Monkey Business*. New York: Dial, 1987.

Boland, Janice. *Annabel*. New York: Dial, 1993.

Bornstein, Ruth. *Little Gorilla*. New York: Seabury, 1976.

Brenner, Anita. *The Boy Who Could Do Anything & Other Mexican Folk Tales*. Hamden, Conn.: Linnet, 1992.

Brett, Jan. *Armadillo Rodeo*. New York: Putnam, 1995.

———. *Goldilocks and the Three Bears*. New York: Dodd, Mead, 1987.

———. *The Mitten*. New York: Putnam, 1989.

———. *The Owl and the Pussycat*. New York: Putnam, 1991.

Bright, Robert. *My Red Umbrella*. New York: Morrow, 1959.

Brown, Anthony. *Gorilla*. New York: Knopf, 1983.

Brown, Marc. *Arthur's Valentine*. Boston: Little, Brown, 1980.

Brown, Margaret Wise. *Animals in the Snow*. New York: Hyperion, 1995.

———. *The Golden Egg Book*. New York: Golden, 1962.

———. *Goodnight Moon*. New York: Harper, 1947.

———. *Nibble, Nibble: Poems for Children*. New York: W. R. Scott, 1959.

Brown, Ruth. *Copycat*. New York: Dutton, 1994.

Bruchac, Joseph. *The First Strawberries*. New York: Dial, 1993.

Bryant, Donna. *My Dog Jessie*. New York: Barron's, 1991.

Buckley, Helen. *Grandfather and I*. New York: Lothrop, Lee & Shepard, 1994.

———. *Grandmother and I*. New York: Lothrop, Lee & Shepard, 1994.

Bunting, Eve. *Flower Garden*. San Diego: Harcourt, 1994.

———. *Ghost's Hour, Spook's Hour*. New York: Clarion, 1987.

———. *The Mother's Day Mice*. New York: Clarion, 1986.

———. *Night Tree*. San Diego: Harcourt, 1991.

———. *A Perfect Father's Day*. New York: Clarion, 1991.

———. *St. Patrick's Day in the Morning*. New York: Houghton Mifflin, 1980.

———. *Sunflower House*. San Diego: Harcourt, 1996.

———. *A Turkey for Thanksgiving*. New York: Clarion, 1991.

———. *The Valentine Bears*. New York: Clarion, 1983.

Burningham, John. *Come Away from the Water, Shirley*. New York: Crowell, 1977.

———. *Mr. Gumpy's Motor Car*. New York: Crowell, 1976.

Butler, Dorothy. *My Brown Bear Barney*. New York: Greenwillow, 1988.

Butterworth, Nick. *My Mom Is Excellent*. Cambridge, Mass.: Candlewick, 1994.

———. *One Snowy Night*. Boston: Little, Brown, 1989.

Caduto, Michael J. *Keepers of the Earth*. Golden, Colo.: Fulcrum, 1988.

Caple, Kathy. *The Coolest Place in Town*. Boston: Houghton Mifflin, 1990.

Carle, Eric. *Do You Want to Be My Friend?* New York: Crowell, 1971.

———. *Papa, Please Get the Moon for Me*. New York: Picture Book Studio USA, 1986.

————. *The Secret Birthday Message.* New York: Crowell, 1972.

Carlson, Nancy. *What If It Never Stops Raining?* New York: Viking, 1992.

Carrick, Carole. *Patrick's Dinosaurs.* New York: Clarion, 1983.

————. *Valentine.* New York: Clarion, 1995.

Casey, Patricia. *Quack, Quack.* New York: Lothrop, Lee & Shepard, 1988.

Cauley, Lorinda Bryan. *Jack and the Beanstalk.* New York: Putnam, 1983.

————. *The Trouble with Tyrannosaurus Rex.* San Diego: Harcourt, 1988.

Chapman, Cheryl. *Snow on Snow on Snow.* New York: Dial, 1994.

Cheng, Hou-Tien. *The Six Chinese Brothers.* New York: Holt, 1979.

Child, Lydia Maria. *Over the River and through the Wood.* Boston: Little, Brown, 1994.

Chocolate, Deborah M. Newton. *My First Kwanzaa Book.* New York: Scholastic, 1992.

Christelow, Eileen. *Five Little Monkeys Sitting in a Tree.* New York: Clarion, 1991.

Chute, Linda. *Clever Tom and the Leprechaun.* New York: Lothrop, Lee & Shepard, 1988.

Clarke, Gus. *Ten Green Monsters.* New York: Western, 1993.

Clifton, Lucille. *Three Wishes.* New York: Delacorte, 1992.

Cocca-Leffler, Maryann. *Wednesday Is Spaghetti Day.* New York: Scholastic, 1990.

Cohen, Carol L. *Wake Up, Groundhog.* New York: Crown, 1975.

Cohen, Miriam. *Bee My Valentine!* New York: Greenwillow, 1978.

Cole, Babette. *Prince Cinders.* New York: Putnam, 1988.

————. *The Trouble with Uncle.* Boston: Little, Brown, 1992.

Conrad, Pam. *Doll Face Has a Party!* New York: HarperCollins, 1994.

————. *The Tub People.* New York: Harper, 1989.

Cooney, Nancy Evans. *The Umbrella Day.* New York: Philomel, 1989.

Coplans, Peta. *Spaghetti for Suzy.* Boston: Houghton Mifflin, 1993.

Crawford, Ron. *Pet?* New York: Green Tiger, 1993.

Crews, Donald. *School Bus.* New York: Greenwillow, 1984.

Croll, Carolyn. *The Little Snowgirl.* New York: Putnam, 1989.

Dale, Penny. *Ten out of Bed.* Cambridge, Mass.: Candlewick, 1994.

Daly, Niki. *Not So Fast, Songololo.* New York: Atheneum, 1986.

Dayrell, Elphinstone. *Why the Sun and Moon Live in the Sky.* Boston: Houghton Mifflin, 1968.

Degen, Bruce. *Jamberry.* New York: Harper, 1983.

Delton, Judy. *Three Friends Find Spring.* New York: Crown, 1977.

————. *Two Good Friends.* New York: Crown, 1974.

Demarest, Chris. *No Peas for Nellie.* New York: Macmillan, 1988.

Demi. *Dragon Kites and Dragonflies: A Collection of Chinese Nursery Rhymes.* San Diego: Harcourt, 1986.

Denim, Sue. *The Dumb Bunnies.* New York: Blue Sky, 1994.

De Paola, Tomie. *Fin M'Coul: The Giant of Knockmany Hill.* New York: Holiday, 1981.

————. *Jamie O'Rourke and the Big Potato.* New York: Putnam, 1991.

————. *Strega Nona.* Englewood Cliffs, N.J.: Prentice-Hall, 1975.

De Regniers, Beatrice Schenk. *May I Bring a Friend?* New York: Atheneum, 1964.

Dexter, Alison. *Grandma*. New York: HarperCollins, 1993.

Douglass, Barbara. *Good as New*. New York: Lothrop, Lee & Shepard, 1982.

Dowling, Paul. *Jimmy's Sunny Book*. New York: Bantam Doubleday Dell, 1994.

Duke, Kate. *Bedtime*. New York: Dutton, 1986.

Dunbar, Joyce. *Four Fierce Kittens*. New York: Scholastic, 1991.

Dupré, Judith. *The Mouse Bride: A Mayan Folk Tale*. New York: Knopf, 1993.

Ehlert, Lois. *Feathers for Lunch*. San Diego: Harcourt, 1990.

———. *Planting a Rainbow*. San Diego: Harcourt, 1988.

Emberly, Ed. *Go Away, Big Green Monster!* Boston: Little, Brown, 1992.

Enderle, Judith Ross. *Six Creepy Sheep*. Honesdale, Pa.: Caroline, 1992.

Evans, Katie. *Hunky Dory Ate It*. New York: Dutton, 1992.

Feeney, Stephanie. *Hawaii Is a Rainbow*. Honolulu: University of Hawaii, 1985.

Field, Eugene. *Wynken, Blynken, and Nod*. New York: Dutton, 1982.

Fowler, Richard. *Cat's Car*. Chicago: Children's, 1988.

Fox, Mem. *Koala Lou*. San Diego: Harcourt, 1988.

———. *Time for Bed*. San Diego: Harcourt, 1993.

———. *Tough Boris*. San Diego: Harcourt, 1994.

Galbraith, Kathryn O. *Laura Charlotte*. New York: Philomel, 1990.

Galdone, Paul. *The Frog Prince*. New York: McGraw-Hill, 1974.

———. *The Teeny-Tiny Woman: A Ghost Story*. New York: Clarion, 1984.

———. *The Three Bears*. New York: Seabury, 1972.

———. *The Three Billy Goats Gruff*. New York: Seabury, 1973.

———. *The Three Little Kittens*. New York: Clarion, 1986.

———. *The Three Little Pigs*. New York: Seabury, 1970.

Gates, Frieda. *Owl Eyes*. New York: Lothrop, Lee & Shepard, 1994.

Geraghty, Paul. *Look Out Patrick!* New York: Macmillan, 1990.

———. *Solo*. New York: Crown, 1995.

Gill, Madelaine. *The Spring Hat*. Englewood Cliffs, N.J.: Silver, 1992.

Ginsburg, Mirra. *Across the Stream*. New York: Greenwillow, 1982.

———. *Asleep, Asleep*. New York: Greenwillow, 1992.

———. *Mushroom in the Rain*. New York: Aladdin, 1990.

———. *Where Does the Sun Go at Night?* New York: Greenwillow, 1981.

Glazer, Tom. *Do Your Ears Hang Low?* Garden City, N.Y.: Doubleday, 1980.

———. *Eye Winker, Tom Tinker, Chin Chopper*. New York: Doubleday, 1973.

Goodspeed, Peter. *A Rhinoceros Wakes Me Up in the Morning*. New York: Puffin, 1984.

Gray, Nigel. *A Country Far Away*. New York: Orchard, 1988.

Greenfield, Eloise. *Grandpa's Face*. New York: Philomel, 1988.

Grifalconi, Ann. *The Village of Round and Square Houses*. Boston: Little, Brown, 1986.

Grossman, Virginia. *Ten Little Rabbits*. San Francisco: Chronicle, 1991.

Guthrie, Donna. *Mrs. Gigglebelly Is Coming for Tea*. New York: Simon & Schuster, 1990.

Hall, Donald. *I Am the Dog, I Am the Cat*. New York: Dial, 1994.

Halpern, Shari. *I Have a Pet!* New York: Macmillan, 1994.

Hellen, Nancy. *The Bus Stop*. New York: Orchard, 1988.

———. *Old MacDonald Had a Farm*. New York: Orchard, 1990.

Hersom, Kathleen. *The Copycat*. New York: Atheneum, 1989.

Hill, Eric. *Spot Goes to the Beach*. New York: Putnam, 1985.

———. *Spot on the Farm*. New York: Putnam, 1985.

———. *Spot's First Christmas*. New York: Putnam, 1983.

———. *Where's Spot?* New York: Puffin, 1994.

Hilton, Nette. *Prince Lachlan*. New York: Orchard, 1990.

Hines, Anna Grossnickle. *Daddy Makes the Best Spaghetti*. New York: Clarion, 1986.

Hissey, Jane. *Jolly Snow*. New York: Philomel, 1991.

Hoban, Julia. *Amy Loves the Rain*. New York: Harper, 1989.

———. *Amy Loves the Sun*. New York: Harper, 1988.

Holl, Adelaide. *The Rain Puddle*. New York: Lothrop, Lee & Shepard, 1965.

Horwitz, Elinor. *When the Sky Is Like Lace*. Philadelphia: Lippincott, 1975.

Hurd, Thacher. *Little Mouse's Big Valentine*. New York: Harper, 1990.

Hutchins, Pat. *Changes, Changes*. New York: Macmillan, 1971.

———. *The Doorbell Rang*. New York: Greenwillow, 1986.

———. *Goodnight Owl*. New York: Aladdin, 1990.

———. *Little Pink Pig*. New York: Greenwillow, 1994.

———. *My Best Friend*. New York: Greenwillow, 1993.

———. *One-Eyed Jake*. New York: Greenwillow, 1979.

———. *Silly Billy*. New York: Greenwillow, 1992.

Inkpen, Mick. *Kipper*. Boston: Little, Brown, 1992.

———. *Kipper's Birthday*. San Diego: Harcourt, 1993.

———. *Kipper's Toybox*. San Diego: Harcourt, 1992.

———. *Lullabyhullaballoo*. New York: Artists and Writers Guild, 1994.

———. *Penguin Small*. San Diego: Harcourt, 1993.

Isadora, Rachel. *At the Crossroads*. New York: Mulberry, 1994.

Jacobs, Joseph. *English Fairy Tales*. New York: Dover, 1967.

Jensen, Kiersten. *Possum in the House*. Milwaukee, Wis.: Gareth Stevens, 1989.

Johnston, Tony. *The Tale of Rabbit and Coyote*. New York: Putnam, 1994.

Joosse, Barbara M. *Mama, Do You Love Me?* San Francisco: Chronicle, 1991.

Kalan, Robert. *Jump, Frog, Jump*. New York: Greenwillow, 1981.

Kasza, Keiko. *A Mother for Choco*. New York: Putnam, 1992.

———. *The Wolf's Chicken Stew*. New York: Putnam, 1987.

Keats, Ezra Jack. *Pet Show!* New York: Aladdin, 1972.

Kellogg, Steven. *The Island of the Skog*. New York: Dial, 1973.

———. *Pecos Bill*. New York: Morrow, 1986.

Kent, Jack. *The Caterpillar and the Polliwog*. New York: Simon & Schuster, 1982.

———. *The Fat Cat*. New York: Parents Magazine, 1971.

———. *Round Robin*. Englewood Cliffs, N.J.: Prentice-Hall, 1982.

Kimmel, Eric. *Anansi and the Moss-Covered Rock*. New York: Holiday, 1988.

King, Bob. *Sitting on the Farm*. New York: Orchard, 1992.

Kirk, David. *Miss Spider's Tea Party*. New York: Callaway, 1994.

Kleven, Elisa. *The Lion and the Little Red Bird*. New York: Dutton, 1992.

Kopper, Lisa. *Daisy Thinks She Is a Baby*. New York: Knopf, 1994.

Kraus, Robert. *The Little Giant*. New York: Harper, 1967.

Krauss, Ruth. *The Carrot Seed*. New York: Harper, 1945.

Kroll, Steven. *It's Groundhog Day!* New York: Holiday, 1987.

Kudrna, Charlene Imbior. *To Bathe a Boa*. Minneapolis: Carolrhoda, 1986.

Lee, Hector Viveros. *I Had a Hippopotamus*. New York: Lee & Low, 1996.

Leman, Martin. *Ten Cats and Their Tales*. New York: Holt, 1981.

Lester, Helen. *The Revenge of the Magic Chicken*. Boston: Houghton Mifflin, 1990.

Lewis, Paul Owen. *P. Bear's New Year's Party!* Pickering, Ont.: S. Mattacchione, 1989.

Lionni, Leo. *Little Blue and Little Yellow*. New York: McDowell, 1959.

Little, Jack. *Once upon a Golden Apple*. Markham, Ont.: Viking Kestrel, 1991.

Lobel, Arnold. *Giant John*. New York: Harper, 1964.

London, Jonathan. *Froggy Learns to Swim*. New York: Viking, 1995.

Luttrell, Ida. *Mattie's Little Possum Pet*. New York: Atheneum, 1993.

MacCarthy, Patricia. *Ocean Parade: A Counting Book*. New York: Dial, 1990.

McDermott, Gerald. *Papagayo the Mischief Maker*. San Diego: Harcourt, 1992.

———. *Tim O'Toole and the Wee Folk*. New York: Viking, 1990.

———. *Zomo the Rabbit: A Trickster Tale from West Africa*. San Diego: Harcourt, 1992.

MacDonald, Golden. *The Little Island*. Garden City, N.Y.: Doubleday, 1946.

MacDonald, Margaret Read. *When the Lights Go Out: Twenty Scary Tales to Tell*. New York: H. W. Wilson, 1988.

McKean, Thomas. *Hooray for Grandma Jo!* New York: Crown, 1994.

MacLachlan, Patricia. *All the Places to Love*. New York: HarperCollins, 1994.

McNaughton, Colin. *Here Come the Aliens!* Cambridge, Mass.: Candlewick, 1995.

McNulty, Faith. *Snake in the House*. New York: Scholastic, 1994.

McPhail, David. *Emma's Pet*. New York: Dutton, 1985.

———. *Pig Pig Grows Up*. New York: Dutton, 1980.

Mallett, David. *Inch By Inch: The Garden Song*. New York: HarperCollins, 1995.

Mann, Pamela. *The Frog Princess*. Milwaukee, Wis.: Gareth Stevens, 1995.

Marshall, Edward. *Space Case*. New York: Dial, 1980.

Martin, Antoinette. *Famous Seaweed Soup*. Morton Grove, Ill.: Whitman, 1993.

Martin, Bill. *Old Devil Wind*. San Diego: Harcourt, 1993.

Martin, David. *Lizzie and Her Puppy*. Cambridge, Mass.: Candlewick, 1993.

Marzollo, Jean. *Sun Song*. New York: HarperCollins, 1995.

Mayer, Mercer. *Cowboy Critter*. New York: Little Simon, 1986.

———. *There's Something in My Attic*. New York: Dial, 1988.

Meddaugh, Susan. *Too Many Monsters*. Boston: Houghton Mifflin, 1982.

Medearis, Angela Shelf. *The Zebra-Riding Cowboy: A Folk Song from the Old West*. New York: Holt, 1992.

Mellor, Corrine. *Clark the Toothless Shark*. New York: Golden, 1994.

Miller, Margaret. *Whose Hat?* New York: Greenwillow, 1988.

Minarik, Else. *It's Spring!* New York: Greenwillow, 1989.

Modell, Frank. *Goodbye Old Year, Hello New Year*. New York: Greenwillow, 1984.

———. *One Zillion Valentines*. New York: Greenwillow, 1981.

Moorman, Margaret. *Light the Lights! A Story about Celebrating Hanukkah and Christmas*. New York: Cartwheel, 1994.

Morgan, Pierr. *The Turnip*. New York: Philomel, 1990.

Morozumi, Atsuko. *One Gorilla*. New York: Farrar, Straus & Giroux, 1990.

Morris, Ann. *The Daddy Book*. Parsippany, N.J.: Silver, 1996.

———. *The Mommy Book*. Parsippany, N.J.: Silver, 1996.

Morris, Winifred. *What if the Shark Wears Tennis Shoes?* New York: Atheneum, 1990.

Mosel, Arlene. *Tikki, Tikki, Tembo*. New York: Holt, 1968.

Most, Bernard. *If the Dinosaurs Came Back*. New York: Harcourt, 1978.

Mullins, Patricia. *Dinosaur Encore*. New York: HarperCollins, 1993.

Munsch, Robert. *Love You Forever*. Scarborough, Ont.: Firefly, 1986.

———. *The Paper Bag Princess*. Toronto: Amnick, 1980.

Newman, Nanette. *There's a Bear in the Bath*. San Diego: Harcourt, 1994.

Nicola-Lisa, W. *1, 2, 3, Thanksgiving*. Morton Grove, Ill.: Whitman, 1991.

Nightingale, Sandy. *A Giraffe on the Moon*. San Diego: Harcourt, 1991.

Nodset, Joan L. *Who Took the Farmer's Hat?* New York: Harper, 1963.

Novak, Matt. *Claude and Sun*. New York: Bradbury, 1987.

Numeroff, Laura Joffe. *Chimps Don't Wear Glasses*. New York: Simon & Schuster, 1995.

———. *If You Give a Mouse a Cookie*. New York: Harper, 1985.

Otto, Carolyn. *Ducks, Ducks, Ducks*. New York: HarperCollins, 1991.

Palatini, Margie. *Piggie Pie*. New York: Clarion, 1995.

Paraskevas, Betty. *Monster Beach*. San Diego: Harcourt, 1995.

Paxton, Tom. *The Marvelous Toy*. New York: Morrow, 1996.

Payne, Emmy. *Katy No-Pocket*. Boston: Houghton Mifflin, 1972.

Pearson, Susan. *Jack and the Beanstalk*. New York: Simon & Schuster, 1989.

Perlman, Janet. *The Emperor Penguin's New Clothes*. New York: Viking, 1995.

Pfister, Marcus. *Penguin Pete, Ahoy!* New York: North-South, 1993.

Polacco, Patricia. *Babushka's Doll*. New York: Simon & Schuster, 1990.

Polushkin, Maria. *Mother, Mother, I Want Another*. New York: Crown, 1978.

Pomerantz, Charlotte. *Piggy in the Puddle*. New York: Macmillan, 1974.

Porter-Gaylord, Laurel. *I Love My Mommy Because*. New York: Dutton, 1991.

Primavera, Elise. *The Three Dots*. New York: Putnam, 1993.

Raffi. *Baby Beluga*. New York: Crown, 1990.

———. *Five Little Ducks*. New York: Crown, 1989.

Raschka, Chris. *Yo! Yes?* New York: Orchard, 1993.

Rayner, Mary. *Mrs. Pig's Bulk Buy*. New York: Atheneum, 1981.

Riddell, Chris. *When the Walrus Comes*. New York: Delacorte, 1989.

Robart, Rose. *The Cake That Mack Ate*. Boston: Atlantic Monthly, 1987.

Robbins, Ken. *Beach Days*. New York: Viking, 1987.

Roberts, Bethany. *Halloween Mice*. New York: Clarion, 1995.

Rockwell, Anne. *First Snowfall*. New York: Aladdin, 1992.

———. *My Spring Robin*. New York: Macmillan, 1989.

Ross, Tony. *The Treasure of Cozy Cove*. New York: Farrar, Straus & Giroux, 1989.

Rounds, Glen. *Cowboys*. New York: Holiday, 1991.

Sadler, Marilyn. *Alistair in Outer Space*. Englewood Cliffs, N.J.: Prentice-Hall, 1984.

Schneider, Rex. *Wide-Mouthed Frog*. Owings Mills, Md.: Stemmer, 1980.

Schotter, Roni. *Hanukkah!* Boston: Joy Street, 1990.

Seeger, Pete. *Abiyoyo*. New York: Aladdin, 1994.

Seuling, Barbara. *The Teeny Tiny Woman: An Old English Tale*. New York: Viking, 1976.

Seuss, Dr. *The Sneeches and Other Stories*. New York: Random House, 1961.

Severn, Jeffrey. *George and His Giant Shadow*. San Francisco: Chronicle, 1990.

Seymour, Peter. *What's at the Beach?* New York: Holt, 1985.

Seymour, Tres. *I Love My Buzzard*. New York: Orchard, 1994.

Sharmat, Marjorie. *Hooray for Father's Day*. New York: Holiday, 1987.

Shaw, Nancy. *Sheep out to Eat*. Boston: Houghton Mifflin, 1992.

Shelby, Anne. *Potluck*. New York: Orchard, 1991.

Sheldon, Dyan. *Whale Song*. New York: Dial, 1990.

Siebert, Diane. *Truck Song*. New York: Crowell, 1984.

Silverman, Erica. *Big Pumpkin*. New York: Macmillan, 1992.

———. *Don't Fidget a Feather*. New York: Macmillan, 1994.

Silverstein, Shel. *Where the Sidewalk Ends*. New York: Harper, 1974.

Sirois, Allen. *Dinosaur Dress Up*. New York: Tambourine, 1992.

Slavin, Bill. *The Cat Came Back*. Morton Grove, Ill.: Whitman, 1992.

Slobodkina, Esphyr. *Caps for Sale*. New York: Harper, 1947.

Smalls, Irene. *Jonathan and His Mommy*. Boston: Little, Brown, 1992.

Smax, William. *Big Pig's Hat*. New York: Dial, 1993.

Smith, William Jay. *Ho for a Hat!* Boston: Joy Street, 1989.

Spurr, Elizabeth. *The Biggest Birthday Cake in the World*. San Diego: Harcourt, 1991.

———. *The Gumdrop Tree*. New York: Hyperion, 1994.

Steptoe, John. *The Story of Jumping Mouse: A Native American Legend*. New York: Lothrop, Lee & Shepard, 1984.

Stevens, Janet. *Coyote Steals the Blanket: A Ute Tale*. New York: Holiday, 1993.

———. *Tops and Bottoms*. San Diego: Harcourt, 1994.

Stickland, Paul. *Dinosaur Roar!* New York: Dutton, 1994.

Stock, Catherine. *Christmas Time.* New York: Aladdin, 1993.

———. *Thanksgiving Treat.* New York: Bradbury, 1990.

Stott, Dorothy. *Little Duck's Bicycle Ride.* New York: Dutton, 1991.

Sturges, Philemon. *Rainsong/Snowsong.* New York: North-South, 1995.

Swamp, Chief Jake. *Giving Thanks: A Native American Good Morning Message.* New York: Lee & Low, 1994.

Tafuri, Nancy. *The Barn Party.* New York: Greenwillow, 1995.

———. *Have You Seen My Duckling?* New York: Greenwillow, 1984.

———. *This Is the Farmer.* New York: Greenwillow, 1994.

Tanis, Joel E. *The Dragon Pack Snack Attack.* New York: Four Winds, 1993.

Thayer, Jane. *The Popcorn Dragon.* New York: Morrow, 1989.

Tompert, Ann. *Nothing Sticks Like a Shadow.* Boston: Houghton Mifflin, 1984.

Trapani, Iza. *The Itsy Bitsy Spider.* New York: Whispering Coyote, 1993.

Tresselt, Alvin. *The Mitten.* New York: Lothrop, 1964.

Trinca, Rod. *One Woolly Wombat.* Brooklyn, N.Y.: Kane/Miller, 1985.

Troughton, Joanna. *How the Birds Changed Their Feathers: A South American Indian Folk Tale.* London, Eng.: Blackie, 1986.

Tucker, Kathy. *Do Pirates Take Baths?* Morton Grove, Ill.: Whitman, 1994.

Van Laan, Nancy. *The Big Fat Worm.* New York: Knopf, 1987.

———. *This Is the Hat: A Story in Rhyme.* Boston: Joy Street, 1992.

Vaughan, Marcia K. *Wombat Stew.* Morristown, N.J.: Silver Burdett, 1984.

Vulliamy, Clara. *Ellen and Penguin.* Cambridge, Mass.: Candlewick, 1993.

Waddell, Martin. *The Big, Big Sea.* Cambridge, Mass.: Candlewick, 1994.

———. *Farmer Duck.* Cambridge, Mass.: Candlewick, 1992.

———. *Owl Babies.* Cambridge, Mass.: Candlewick, 1992.

———. *The Pig in the Pond.* Cambridge, Mass.: Candlewick, 1992.

———. *The Toymaker.* Cambridge, Mass.: Candlewick, 1992.

Walsh, Ellen. *Mouse Count.* San Diego: Harcourt, 1991.

Ward, Cindy. *Cookie's Week.* New York: Putnam, 1988.

Watson, Wendy. *Has Winter Come?* London, Eng.: Collins, 1978.

Wells, Rosemary. *Forest of Dreams.* New York: Dial, 1988.

———. *Max's Christmas.* New York: Dial, 1986.

———. *Peabody.* New York: Dial, 1983.

West, Colin. *"Not Me!" Said the Monkey.* New York: Lippincott, 1987.

Westcott, Nadine. *The Giant Vegetable Garden.* Boston: Little, Brown, 1981.

Whybrow, Ian. *Quacky Quack-Quack!* New York: Four Winds, 1991.

Wieser, David. *Tuesday.* New York: Clarion, 1991.

Willis, Jeanne. *Earthlets, As Explained by Professor Xargle.* New York: Dutton, 1989.

Wolkstein, Diane. *The Magic Wings: A Tale from China.* New York: Dutton, 1983.

Wood, Audrey. *The Little Penguin's Tale.* San Diego: Harcourt, 1989.

———. *The Napping House*. San Diego: Harcourt, 1984.

———. *Piggies*. San Diego: Harcourt, 1991.

———. *Silly Sally*. San Diego: Harcourt, 1991.

Wood, Jakki. *Moo, Moo, Brown Cow*. San Diego: Harcourt, 1992.

———. *One Bear with Bees in His Hair*. New York: Dutton, 1990.

Wright, Dare. *The Lonely Doll*. Garden City, N.Y.: Doubleday, 1957.

Wu, Norbert. *Fish Faces*. New York: Holt, 1993.

Yolen, Jane. *Mouse's Birthday*. New York: Putnam, 1993.

Yorinks, Arthur. *Whitefish Will Rides Again*. New York: HarperCollins, 1994.

Young, Ruth. *A Trip to Mars*. New York: Orchard, 1990.

Zacharias, Thomas, and Wanda Zacharias. *But Where Is the Green Parrot?* New York: Delacorte, 1990.

Zelinsky, Paul O. *Wheels on the Bus*. New York: Dutton, 1990.

Ziefert, Harriet. *In a Scary Old House*. New York: Puffin, 1989.

Zimmerman, Andrea. *The Cow Buzzed*. New York: HarperCollins, 1993.

DISCOGRAPHY OF SONGS AND TUNES

"Abiyoyo." Seeger, Pete. *Abiyoyo and Other Story Songs for Children*. Smithsonian/Folkways, 1989.

"Aiken Drum." Raffi. *Singable Songs for the Very Young*. MCA Records, 1976.

"All the Pretty Little Horses." Bartels, Joanie. *Lullaby Magic*. Discovery Music, 1990.

"Auld Lang Syne." Coulter, Phil. *Scottish Tranquility*. Shanachie, 1991.

"The Bear Went over the Mountain." *Wee Sing Silly Songs*. Price, Stern, Sloan, 1986.

"Bingo." Sharon, Lois, and Bram. *Sing A to Z*. Elephant Records, 1990.

"Blow the Man Down." *Wee Sing America*. Price, Stern, Sloan, 1987.

"Buffalo Gals." *Musical Memories of Laura Ingalls Wilder*. Hear and Learn Publications, 1992.

"Car, Car Song." Penner, Fred. *Ebeneezer Sneezer*. Oak St. Music, 1991.

"Do Your Ears Hang Low?" *Wee Sing Silly Songs*. Price, Stern, Sloan, 1986.

"Eensy Weensy Spider." Sharon, Lois, and Bram. *Mainly Mother Goose*. Elephant Records, 1984.

"Farmer in the Dell." *Wee Sing and Play*. Price, Stern, Sloan, 1986.

"Five Little Frogs." Raffi. *Singable Songs for the Very Young*. MCA Records, 1976.

"For He's a Jolly Good Fellow." *All Occasions Album*. Gateway Records, 1982.

"Frère Jacques." Raffi. *Corner Grocery Store*. MCA Records, 1979.

"The Garden Song." *Peter, Paul, and Mommy Too*. Warner Brothers, 1993.

"The Green Grass Grew All Around." Seeger, Pete. *Abiyoyo and Other Story Songs for Children*. Smithsonian/Folkways, 1989.

"Hanukkah Song." *Hanukkah, Oh Hanukkah!* Kar-Ben Copies, Inc., 1995.

"Happy Birthday to You." Sharon, Lois, and Bram. *Happy Birthday*. Elephant Records, 1988.

"Happy Trails." *The Cowboy Album*. Kid Rhino, 1992.

"Here We Go 'Round the Mulberry Bush." *Sing Along Songs*. Warner Brothers, 1992.

"The Hokey Pokey." Bartels, Joanie. *Dancin' Magic*. Discovery Music, 1991.

"Home on the Range." *The Cowboy Album*. Kid Rhino, 1992.

"I'm a Little Teapot." Hammett, Carol. *Preschool Action Time*. Kimbo Educational, 1988.

"I'm Being Swallowed by a Boa Constrictor." Peter, Paul, and Mary. *Peter, Paul, and Mommy*. Warner Brothers, 1969.

"I'm Bringing Home a Baby Bumblebee." *Wee Sing Silly Songs*. Price, Stern, Sloan, 1986.

"It's Raining, It's Pouring." Peter, Paul, and Mary. *Peter, Paul, and Mommy*. Warner Brothers, 1969.

"Kookaburra." *Wee Sing Sing-Alongs*. Price, Stern, Sloan, 1982.

"La Raspa." (The Mexican Hat Dance Song) Jenkins, Ella. *Little Johnny Brown*. Smithsonian/Folkways Records, 1990.

"Lavender's Blue." *Moonbeams & Gentle Dreams*. Music for Little People, 1991.

"London Bridge." *Sing Along Songs*. Warner Brothers Records, 1992.

"Marvelous Toy." Peter, Paul, and Mary. *Peter, Paul, and Mommy*. Warner Brothers, 1969.

"Mary Wore Her Red Dress." Seeger, Mike, and Peggy Seeger. *American Folk Songs for Children*. Rounder Records, 1987.

"Monster Mash." *Halloween Hits*. Rhino, 1991.

"The More We Get Together." *Sing Along Songs*. Warner Brothers, 1992.

"Mr. Sun." Raffi. *Singable Songs for the Very Young*. MCA Records, 1976.

"My Bonnie Lies Over the Ocean." Lansky, Vicki. *Vicki Lansky's Sing Along as You Ride Along*. Scholastic, 1988.

*"Nuts in May." Hart, Jane. *Singing Bee!* New York: Lothrop, Lee & Shepard Books, 1982.

"Octopus's Garden." The Beatles. Apple Records, 1969.

"The Old Chisholm Trail." *The Cowboy Album*. Kid Rhino, 1992.

"Old MacDonald." Hart, Jane. *Singing Bee!* New York: Lothrup, 1982.

"On Top of Spaghetti." Little Richard. *Shake It All About*. Disney, 1992.

"Over the River and through the Wood." Disney Travel Songs. Walt Disney Records, 1994.

"Peanut Butter and Jelly." Sharon, Lois, and Bram. *Smorgasbord*. Elephant Records, 1980.

"Peanut on a Railroad Track." *Wee Sing Silly Songs*. Price, Stern, Sloan, 1986.

"Rags." Sharon, Lois, and Bram. *Great Big Hits*. Elephant Records, 1992.

---

* Print source

"Riding in My Car." Seeger, Pete. *Children's Concert at Town Hall.* Columbia, 1990.

"Row Row Row Your Boat." *Wee Sing Sing-Alongs.* Price, Stern, Sloan, 1982.

"Sing a Song of Sixpence." *Wee Sing King Cole's Party.* Price, Stern, Sloan, 1987.

"Six Little Ducks." Raffi. *More Singable Songs.* MCA Records, 1977.

"Ten in the Bed." *Wee Sing Silly Songs.* Price, Stern, Sloan, 1986.

"Too-ra-loo-ra." Day, Dennis. *My Wild Irish Rose.* RCA Records, 1986.

"Twinkle, Twinkle, Little Star." Raffi. *One Light, One Sun.* MCA Records, 1985.

"Under the Sea." *Disney's Sebastian: From The Little Mermaid.* Disney, 1990.

"We Wish You a Merry Christmas." *Tomie de Paola's Book of Christmas Carols.* Listening Library, 1988.

"Wheels on the Bus." Raffi. *Rise and Shine.* MCA Records, 1982.

Diane Briggs is a youth services librarian at the Bethlehem Public Library in Delmar, New York, a school media specialist at the Maplewood School in Watervliet, New York, and a member of the National Storytelling Association. A graduate of the School of Information Science at the State University of New York at Albany, Briggs is also the author of *Flannel Board Fun* and *Toddler Storytime Programs,* both published by Scarecrow Press. Briggs lives in Delmar, New York, with her husband Scott and son Thomas.

Photo by Lynn Finley